At Peace with Money

A Holistic Roadmap to Financial Wellness

CARRIE FRIEDBERG
SF Money Coach

Post Hill Press

A POST HILL PRESS BOOK
ISBN: 979-8-88845-769-6
ISBN (eBook): 979-8-88845-770-2

At Peace with Money:
A Holistic Roadmap to Financial Wellness

Cover design by Jim Villaflores

This book, as well as any other Post Hill Press publications, may be purchased in bulk quantities at a special discounted rate. Contact orders@posthillpress.com for more information.

Post Hill Press
New York • Nashville
posthillpress.com

Published in the United States of America
1 2 3 4 5 6 7 8 9 10

Advance Praise for *At Peace with Money*

"*At Peace with Money* stands out among personal finance books. In this captivating read, Carrie Friedberg offers unique, honest, and fresh advice on managing your cash flow. When you're ready to face your emotions around money and take financial control, this book is for you!"

—Barbara Huson, author of *Overcoming Underearning* and *Rewire for Wealth*

"Finally, a book that imparts deep, lasting insights about money from a truly holistic perspective. If your money mojo is not what you want it to be, reading *At Peace with Money* will feel like having your own personal financial advisor and therapist in your hands. A delightful blend of specific tactics for managing your finances and raw explorations of the myriad of emotions that money triggers—your left and right brain will thank you for reading this delightful book!"

—Manisha Thakor, MBA, CFA, CFP®, author of *MoneyZen: The Secret to Finding Your Enough*

"At last, a finance book that addresses both the practical and the psychological hurdles that can keep us from experiencing ease and flow with money. Carrie Friedberg shares generously from her personal financial wellness journey and delivers actionable advice that has worked for her and for her hundreds of coaching clients over the years. This will definitely go on my recommended reading list!"

—Kerri Kimball, CFP®, SCRIC®,
managing partner of Apogee Wealth Advisors

"*At Peace with Money* is a game changer for anyone looking to transform their relationship with money. Carrie Friedberg brilliantly combines practical tools, actionable systems, and a holistic approach to create a roadmap for financial success. Whether you're balancing work and family, teaching your kids about money, or simply trying to find peace in your financial life, this book is packed with wisdom and advice. It's not just about dollars and cents—it's about creating a life of balance, clarity, and abundance."

—Joshua Cooper, CPA of Tax Lovin'

For Lucy, Max, and Andrew,
the greatest loves of my life

Table of Contents

Foreword by Dr. Brad Klontz, PsyD, CFP®

Managing personal finances is more than just crunching numbers or sticking to a budget. It's about understanding the profound ways in which money is woven into every aspect of your life: your relationships, your health, your sense of purpose, and your emotional well-being. Too often, we reduce money to a transactional tool—something we use to pay bills or accumulate wealth. But what if we reframed money as a powerful resource for creating a life of meaning and fulfillment? What if your day to day financial decisions were deeply aligned with your vision for the future?

At Peace with Money is more than just another personal finance book. It can help you transform the way in which you think about money. It invites you to step away from traditional views of finance and embrace a holistic approach, one that acknowledges the connection between your financial life and your emotional, physical, and even spiritual health. True wealth isn't just about the number in your bank account; it's about the experiences you are having and the life you are building.

It's about aligning your financial choices with your deepest aspirations.

In *At Peace with Money*, you'll learn to connect your financial behaviors with your values. Whether you're just starting your financial journey or simply looking for fresh insights, this book offers practical tools and mindset shifts to help you take control of your money. We live in a time when people are searching for more than just material success. My hope is that this book inspires you to redefine wealth in a way that resonates with your authentic self.

—Dr. Brad Klontz, PsyD, CFP®
Financial psychologist and national
bestselling author of *Start Thinking Rich*

Dear Reader,

Throughout this book, I chose to use she/her and he/him pronouns, but you're encouraged to replace them with pronouns that resonate with you. Also, a heads up that I use the word God interchangeably with Higher Power and the Universe. It feels necessary to me to include this language in my story, but feel free to replace the word God with anything outside of yourself. What follows is a holistic personal finance road map based on my own financial wellness journey and professional experience coaching clients ages twenty-two to seventy-seven across twenty-three states and five continents over the last two decades. The Universe has your back and I'm here as your guide.

Love, Carrie

Preface

At the time, many of my friends—bolstered by their Saturn returns—were getting married, purchasing homes, and having babies. Resistant to adulting in my late twenties, I spent most of my time, energy, and money on my free-range lifestyle—including personal development, all-night dance parties, bodywork, traveling, and vast amounts of time in nature ingesting MDMA (ecstasy) or psilocybin (mushrooms), depending on the weekend.[1] I moved to San Francisco after college and had quickly become a self-help junkie participating in Reiki trainings, transformational communication courses, holotropic breathwork, Gestalt inquiry workshops, sacred rituals in women's circles, purifying fire ceremonies, getting certified as a yoga instructor, learning to meditate, and becoming a "graduate" of the Landmark Worldwide Curriculum for Living (formerly Erhard Seminars Training, or EST). While all of these experiences were additive, they were also expensive. I had a much

1 I do not condone or encourage any behavior involving plant medicine, illicit, or illegal drugs unless it is prescribed by a medical doctor, substances are tested, you're at least twenty-six years old (with a fully developed adult brain), and the use occurs in a licensed therapeutic or medical setting with a focus on integration.

bigger vision for my life than I could afford on a teacher's salary, landing me in deep trouble financially. I lived with credit card debt and constant anxiety about money and often succumbed to compulsive spending—like the time I took a spontaneous trip to Italy for three weeks in an attempt to break up with someone. I suffered crippling codependence in my relationships with roommates, friends, colleagues, and family members, and avoided conflict—especially about money—at all costs.

While I was finding myself and seeking enlightenment on the West Coast, my family was being torn apart by rampant alcoholism back home in the Midwest. My own lifehad long been affected by the family disease of alcoholism. In high school, my first boyfriend was a heavy drinker, which started a long string of intimate relationships with people whose first love was alcohol. My mom, who passed away from cancer in 2018, was a lifelong daily drinker. Other members of my family earned DUI (driving under the influence) citations, arrests, hospitalizations, and public humiliations in our small preppy community. One relative even attended residential rehab for addiction to alcohol over ten times.

The obsession, excessive sense of responsibility, fear of failure, overfunctioning, and failed attempts at controlling others took a toll on my health, ability to work, and relationships. My thinking became distorted, and I spent much of my life energy stressed, worried, and trying to fix everyone. The grief was all-consuming and eventually brought me to my knees.

The day my latest boyfriend told me he "*slept on the kitchen floor last night in a blackout*," I attended my first meeting of Al-Anon for friends and family of alcoholics. Indeed, my life had become *unmanageable*. I went to the program because of "them," but I stayed because of me. The program helped me in countless visible and invisible ways. Whether "they" were still drinking or not, serenity, *passaddhi* in Sanskrit, began seeping back into my heart and mind. I gained emotional maturity and developed a sense of inner peace. And the slogans, steps, principles, and traditions of the Al-Anon program have been a significant part of my life and internal makeup ever since.

Back in California, after a series of *almost* engagements, I managed to fall hopelessly in love with Marc, who was thirteen years my senior. I dove in, quick and steep, and immediately started helping him raise his two girls, ages three and four. Now in my early thirties, I was ready to settle down, and so badly wanted to get married and start a family of my own that I ignored the glaring red flags. Marc was a sober alcoholic with an actual shopping addiction. He was in recovery and I was in recovery, so I convinced myself it would be different this time. However, he was a clotheshorse and spent obscene amounts of money on high-end clothes, shoes, and watches, which was as baffling and crazy-making as counting an alcoholic's drinks. Collection agencies called the landline all day long. He trained me to run interference. A huge pile of his unopened mail overflowed from a bowl on the landing. Marc told me to mind my own business. Pacific Gas and Electric turned the power off. He exclaimed, "Everyone makes mistakes!" and quickly paid the overdue bill to put the lights back on.

I agonized over the future of the relationship, and every time I wanted to have a heart-to-heart, he shut me down and refused to talk. And then, long after I moved in, Marc confessed he had over $200,000 of personal credit card debt from spending the money on his bachelor pad postdivorce as well as his "little spending issue." Yet, I gave him my own credit card to use for "work trips." He used and abused my credit card, repeatedly promising me he'd pay it off, but never could and never did. I was also financially dependent on him, living in a penthouse apartment in Pacific Heights—which we couldn't afford. I stuck my head in the sand, loved him with abandon, and enjoyed his nonstop lavish gifts like first-class plane tickets, front-row concert tickets, access to exclusive clubs, weekends away at Post Ranch Inn, fine jewelry, and wardrobe upgrades.

The day before we were scheduled to depart on a trip to Hawaii, a longtime dream of mine and the chance to celebrate my birthday, Marc confessed that instead of buying the engagement ring we had shopped for, he blew the money on more clothes for himself. And I insisted we keep our plans and go on the trip the next day. Our assumed engagement trip was tense and terrible, but *I still wanted it to work*, even though he was obviously self-destructing and sabotaging our relationship. Yet, I remained complicit, and my denial was still thick until, upon return, a couples therapist sternly yelled, "*Don't you see you're part of the problem*?" I was jolted out of the fantasy that I was living an authentically wealthy lifestyle and was going to marry this guy. My heart stung and instantly hardened as three years of magical thinking shattered into a thousand pieces, and I realized it was over. After we drove home in silence, I slept in another room, heaving in emotional pain. My dreams were crumbling. The naive little girl inside of me died that night, and my wiser feminine essence awakened. As is commonly spoken in Buddhist circles, *attachment causes suffering.* I needed to let go and let God.

After all of the crazy money experiences with Marc, I realized it was time to face the final frontier: money. I unabashedly launched myself into a financial wellness journey. I set out on a mission to earn more money, get educated in the realm of personal finance, heal my nonexistent self-esteem, and stop accepting the unacceptable. One day later, I was hired as a chief of staff for an affluent family in the city, earning more than I ever had as a teacher. Miracle! *Thank you, God, Good Orderly Direction, and the Universe for ALWAYS having my back.* The next phase of my healing took a while, but starting with a beginner's mind, step by step, I learned the ABCs and 123s of personal finance with the help of a money coach. I studied, practiced, read multiple series of personal finance books, watched lectures and attended seminars about money, hired a traditional financial therapist, stumbled, and persevered. After being on a high-speed train to financial ruin, I was called off the train. The breakup, which happened soon after I started getting right with my own money, didn't surprise anyone. My dear friend Alicia took me out for breakfast and seared me with a truth bomb: "You dodged a bullet." I was now thirty-five years old and single, *again*.

It dawned on me that maybe I could become a money coach. I had a background in education, and the more I thought about it, the more it made sense. I would still be teaching, but with different content and a different audience. Plus, my intuition was saying, "YES, YES, YES!" And so, after two years of financial recovery, I decided to do the same counselor training program that my own coach had done and a subsequent Financial Behavior Specialist® certification program. Over the course of fifteen years since then, I have developed a holistic personal finance curriculum with tons of practical tools and inspiration based on myl experiences with the Law of Attraction, personal and professional research, brain-science theories, and cognitive behavioral therapy techniques. I can't promise the journey of financial wellness will be easy for you the entire time, but I've broken it down into bite-size, actionable steps. As one of my favorite clients said to me, "I need you to talk to me like a five-year-old!" If you keep an open mind, you will see there is low-hanging fruit all around you. Take what is relevant to your situation and leave the rest. If I can do it, you, too, can alter your relationship with money forever.

I won't deceive you. I grew up with privilege. I am not a trust fund baby, but I had safety, security, a nicely appointed home with warm food for dinner every night, and even some luxuries in my childhood and teenage years. My parents loved me unconditionally and cared for me on every level as best they could. They graciously introduced me to spirituality too. From a young age, being immersed in sacred experiences seemed normal. Every night, my parents said prayers with me at bedtime. Every Sunday morning, they took us four kids to Christ Church Grosse Pointe for breakfast, the service, and Sunday school. I grew up in the church. We were all baptized and confirmed there, and I attended the youth groups, sang in the choir, and was an acolyte. Looking back, all of these church experiences were positive and really opened up my life to a divine flow. True to "the rubber band theory," I took two decades off from church attendance, but my kids are now finally old enough to sit for a little while in the sanctuary before happily running off to Sunday school with their amazing teachers. I am back at church almost every week, and it feels like home. As written about in the book by Lisa Miller, PhD, *The Spiritual Child*, nurturing my connection with a Higher Power was probably the single most powerful and important gift my parents ever gave me.

Regardless of that foundation, I still had to fight, scratch, and crawl my way through a long, trying journey of financial recovery. Due to my widely meandering path in early adulthood, it took hard work to untangle and reset my relationship with money. I had been enshrouded by money fog—a form of denial and an act of keeping yourself small and confused. I fantasized about the old days of *just swiping the card*. Believe me, I looked for the escape hatch, but there was no easier, softer way. Getting honest with myself was horribly painful at times, and I wanted so badly to quit, go back to oblivion, and hide from it all. The journey of healing my relationship with money was complicated and demanding, but I looked in the mirror one day and said aloud, "You deserve to be happy." I had to grow up and start living within my means.

At Peace with Money is the culmination of everything I have learned since that excruciating realization that there must be a better way. For me, I had to change everything about how I dealt with money. In this book, I've recorded the insights I received and lessons I learned along the way, including essential personal finance tools and routines. I've created a plan that works to move past scarcity, shame, overwhelm, financial illiteracy, and any other obstacles in the way of your balanced, prosperous, and best life.

I wrote this book to offer hope for a life beyond money fog and magical thinking. To share a holistic approach, with a wide range of experiences and practical solutions to everyday money problems. To help reduce stress and increase your sense of well-being. To share that if you summon enough courage to ask, help is readily available. So you can avoid landing in my office one day feeling like a shred of yourself, or facing even more serious consequences.

I believe in a world where all people have access to financial education and tools so they can thrive and contribute to society in positive ways. Whatever your circumstances, there are solutions. And, no matter how deep the chaos runs, it never has to get worse than it is today. This book is for everyone—from young adults to retirees in all stages of wealth: survival mode, financial stability, and affluence. Step by step, I have written out a guide to success with personal finance through practices of awareness, acceptance, and action. Whenever my husband, Andrew, asks how my workday was, I respond, "Slaying dragons and changing lives!" This book is preventive medicine for YOU and your loved ones. *And so it is.*

Introduction

Grounding Meditation

Close your eyes and take four deep breaths. Take an inventory of your body, and make note of any place you are experiencing pain or tension. Send your breath to any blocked areas, and allow the tension to release. Take your time in doing this so you can truly allow your body to relax.

Imagine yourself going to a place you love in nature, where you feel very filled up with energy. The thought of this place brings you a sense of calm and joy. Walk around, expanding your vision 360 degrees, and take in all you see. Allow yourself to really feel being in this place. Feel the air on your skin. Is it wet or dry, warm or cold? Feel your feet on the ground, and wiggle your toes in the earth. Touch the earth. Listen to all the sounds. Do you hear water running or the wind blowing? Are there sounds of life here, or is it very still? Smell all the smells.

Now look around and find a tree you can sit with. Ask the tree permission to sit with it for a while, and if it says yes, sit down on the ground, leaning your back against the tree and feel the solid support you have. Take a symbolic journey inside the tree, starting with the root system. Imagine being able to suck water up through your roots, bringing nutrients to every part of the tree and through your entire body. Feel how you start to pulsate with life and energy as each cell is being fed. Allow that energy to move throughout your body as you experience it moving through the trunk of the tree, into its branches, and through your own extremities, feeding the leaves and the fruit that represent life—feeling your life. Feel your connection with all of life. You are part of a greater whole. None of us is here alone.

Really lean back into the tree and experience the love of the Universe. Know that you are, right now, being given guidance on how to find the tools to bring you to a place of wholeness.

Reprinted with permission from Sandra Ingerman's *Soul Retrieval: Mending the Fragmented Self*

Keys to Success

Along with having fifth-grade math skills, people who prosper on the path to financial wellness are Honest, Open-minded, and Willing; that is HOW to win at this game. Isn't that wonderful news?

> "Good human qualities...honesty, sincerity, a good heart, cannot be bought with money, nor can they be produced by machines, but only by the mind itself. We call this the inner light, or God's blessing, or human quality. This is the essence of mankind."
>
> —His Holiness the Dalai Lama, Buddhist monk and political/spiritual leader of Tibet

Let's start by discussing honesty. You must be willing to tell yourself—and your loved ones—the truth about your financial life. People closest to you, like family and close friends, can support you in achieving your goals. Self-awareness and honesty have long been pillars of the spiritual path. Bring an attitude of curiosity, and we can figure this out!

Open-mindedness means starting from a blank slate where anything is possible. Like a Phoenix rising, I was open to considering and accepting new ideas, perspectives, and information. Critically, I was also open to asking for and receiving help. When I set out on a mission to change my relationship with money, I shocked myself by completing personal finance books and hiring someone on Craigslist to tutor me in setting up and using Quicken, personal finance software.

At the suggestion of a friend, I even hired a traditional financial therapist. The therapist immediately suggested that I go on a thirty-day cash-only diet. I was absolutely floored. But desperate and seeking my therapist's approval, I was willing to try anything new and healthy sounding. It turned out that writing and mailing checks for billswas a very different experience from forgetting you ever paid for something. Paying with cash at the gas station and asking for a separate check at group dinners was humbling. It felt like wearing someone else's clothes, but inside, I was proud of myself. I have to admit she was onto something, and paying with actual cash rather than just swiping or tapping the card made me more present with my spending choices than I had ever been in my life.

Once I got a taste of financial wellness in that short experiment, I was sold. Next, I decided to close all seven of my store credit cards. I know what you're thinking. *Closing credit cards can negatively affect your credit score.* But I needed closure and control. I didn't have anything on the near-term radar like moving, applying for a job, or buying a car where my credit might be checked, so I followed my instincts. Simplifying my financial life actually felt amazing, even liberating. Then, my therapist suggested I cancel all of my automatic payments. I was forced to take inventory of where my money was going. This quickly propelled me into the driver's seat of my financial life, and I no longer felt like a victim all the time. In the many years since then and as my financial life stabilized I have, of course mindfully reinstated some automatic payments. And, I still refuse to open store cards to this day.

Financial Psychology Research

Extroversion, agreeableness, conscientiousness, neuroticism, and openness to experience had statistically significant positive or negative earnings effects.

I love the Collins dictionary definition of willing, the "W" in HOW. If someone is *willing* to do something, they are fairly happy about doing it, and will do it if they are asked or required to. When it comes to money, you need to be willing not only to examine your behavior, but to also set limits, say "NO," and learn to manage the relentless pressure to consume.

Much to my ego's dismay, after the thirty-day cash diet, my financial therapist led me through some emotional release work around family history. She invited me to fire my "primary money manager model," a.k.a. my dad, whose parents had immigrated to the United States from Germany and lived through the Great Depression. Through tears and heartache, I wrote the letter. I told my dad all the ways in which I felt financially disempowered in our family, along with naming his apparent values and behavior around money that I refused to emulate. I never sent it, that wasn't the point, but it was extremely cathartic to read aloud to my therapist. Around that time, she also encouraged me to take full ownership over an investment account where my dad was still the custodian, a decade longer than he legally needed to be, and that exercise also boosted my confidence.

The therapist asked about my family history, listened to my money stories, and helped me unpack the SHAME, the belief that I Should Have Already Mastered Everything. Prior to that, I had never told anyone about my teenage shoplifting sprees and how I lived for so many years as a codependent, financially-illiterate adult. She urged me to clean up the wreckage of those years and forgive myself for all of the mistakes along the way. Coincidentally, I was on Step 9 in Al-Anon at the time, so I was prepared and ready to make direct amends. My therapist held a loving, safe space for the uncontrollable tears that poured out during every session. Financial therapy felt good and supportive, but I did not learn the first thing about how to create and manage a budget. I was still a mess—and so was my money. I remained totally unequipped to handle my financial life. After six months of emotional labor, I had zero practical skills and was still losing sleep due to constant anxiety about overdraft fees, uncashed checks, and bill due dates, so I quit and quickly reverted to overspending. Her office was on Therapists' Row, after all, Sacramento Street, and littered with expensive boutiques calling my name. I had never paid a hundred dollars for a T-shirt before! I resumed heavy credit card use and exaggerated lies like, "Sure, let's get a ski house for the winter!" and "Yes, I can buy the furniture for our apartment!" and "I'll just pay for it and everyone can pay me back!" and "You don't have enough? No problem, I'll just pay more!"

When I hired a financial coach, I finally found what I had been searching for all those years. For the first time in my life, I had a reliable source of financial education, empowerment, and accountability. I was finally able to gain practical skills and learn how to align my spending, saving, and earning with my values. Healing my relationship with money, an outcome of consistent one-on-one financial coaching sessions, completely altered the course of my life. It took me two years to rearrange my spending habits, integrate new knowledge about personal finance, and shift my mindset from stress and negativity to ease and hope. I forgave myself, my parents, and others who had taken advantage of my naivety, and *moved on*. Without the ball and chain of regret and self-hatred, I was able to see possibility again. Ultimately, I learned the importance of telling the truth and how to practice self-care and, in turn, discovered ,that I am not, and never was, alone. Everything changed inside and out. I was able to turn in my dented beater car and get one in far better shape. I moved into a nicer, bigger apartment. These material changes definitely increased my sense of contentment and satisfaction. But perhaps the most surprising and profound benefit of my hard work was the change in my relationships. I had developed a financial acumen and was more confident, forthcoming, and savvy in all of my conversations about money, whether at home with roommates, in friendships, or in romantic relationships. I even showed up differently at work, which meant I negotiated successfully for a higher salary. I stopped overspending on other people and things I didn't need. I started addressing areas of deprivation. With my newfound self-esteem, I was even able to participate in family meetings and conversations about money with my parents and three siblings without going deaf, numb, or bursting into tears. Balance was restored.

Financial Psychology Research

Not surprisingly, higher levels of financial knowledge, including knowledge around issues related to credit, savings, investments, and mortgages, are associated with engagement in prudent financial behaviors such as paying bills on time and having emergency savings.

Who Needs Money Coaching?

There are myriad reasons people hire a money coach. When I dared to call my first financial coach, here are some things I shared:

I want to feel at peace with money.
I can't save five dollars for five minutes.
I have dreams I can't afford.
I get disoriented and my hearing goes out in conversations about money.
I put other people's needs ahead of my own.
I can't stop crying about money.
I have health and relationship problems.
I need to make more money.
My parents fought constantly about money.
I don't have a clue how to budget. I need to start at square one.
I want to act like an adult with money.
I want to stop dating people who are dysfunctional with money, so I need to clean up my side of the street.
I can't continue living like this.

I wrote this book, created a Personal Finance 101 master class, and started a podcast because I am well aware that one-on-one financial coaching is not affordable or otherwise workable for most people. With all my heart, I want you to have access to this information, this medicine. In fifteen years of private practice, I've seen people ask for help both proactively and reactively. The most common reasons people reach out to financial professionals are due to challenges in these areas:

Spending

Saving
Earning
Emotions
Relationships
Family history
Giving
Aging and health
Planning
Debt management
Financial trauma
General help

My hope and intention in sharing the following quotes from actual clients is that you will find something that resonates. I'm certain you will if you *look for the similarities*. This is what they said when I asked, "What brought you into money coaching?"

Spending

I spend too much money on other people and I do it for attention and love.

It's hard to spend money on myself.

I overspend and am always in the red.

My financial advisor told me I need to reduce my spending by $100,000 a year.

I'm in a personal black hole of constant extravagant overspending and lack of discipline.

I need a reality check on my spending.

We need to figure out where our money is going.

I want to keep my horse, but between her feed, boarding, training, equipment, farrier, insurance, and healthcare needs, the costs are becoming prohibitive and I'm struggling to make it all work.

I'm obsessed with deals and unique gifts and other things I don't need on the QVC channel and it's out of control.

I want to be more mindful and joyful about spending money.

Saving

Every year, tax season is a crisis.

We want to be able to pay for private education all the way through.

I drained my IRA to pay for my divorce.

I want to make sure I'm doing everything I can for my future.

I want to build a $100,000 nest egg.

I'm good at making and spending money, but I'm terrible at saving.

Earning

I'm making more money than I ever have.

I make a good amount of money, but it doesn't feel like enough.

I've been the primary caretaker for my ninety-three-year-old father for the last five years. I'm financially dependent on him. And I don't have an income plan for after he dies.

I want to develop multiple streams of passive income.

We're struggling to manage our fluctuating income.

I got laid off.

I'm not good with invoicing. I make do and live without rather than asking to be paid.

I'm a bit of a workaholic and I never feel like I have or make enough money.

I have been living on disability and need to get back into the workforce.

Emotions

My anxiety about money is keeping me up at night.
My head is in the sand.
I live with a feeling of impending doom.
Money is a source of constant stress.
I want to heal the state of deprivation I live in.
I need to learn to sit in the discomfort that comes with facing my finances.
I want to reduce my anxiety about money.
I want to explore my triggers and the root causes of my money issues.
I'm scared to look at my bank account.
I feel frustrated, lost, and confused and have incredible shame and fear about money.
I carry an overwhelming fear that with one wrong decision, I will end up homeless.
Money is very emotional for me.

Relationships

I can't trust my spouse with money.
I delegated too much of our household financial responsibility to my husband and I need to wake up.
I'm experiencing extreme conflict with my partner about money.
I want to manifest a solid financial partnership.
I'm a spender. He's a saver.
My husband was born with some kind of money gene that I don't have.

My partner and I have different attitudes and goals around money and we've created a situation that's out of control.

I filed for divorce.

I live an extravagant lifestyle funded by a man I no longer want to be with.

We're disillusioning our prenup.

We're in mediation to create a postnup.

We're getting married and want to merge our money.

We want to experience ease and flow with communication around money.

We want to get on the same page about money.

Family

I never learned anything useful or positive from my parents about money.

My dad married my mom, who was 100 percent trailer trash, and then founded one of the big five tech companies in Silicon Valley. My beliefs and behaviors around money are conflicted.

I am living off inherited wealth and want to create something of my own.

I want to provide healthy financial modeling for my kids.

I grew up with teenage parents in low-income housing.

I am choosing to break deep patterns of financial dysfunction in my family history.

We never talked about money growing up. We had no money to talk about.

When our parents died, a sibling rivalry turned into litigation over the inheritance.

I work really hard here in the States and send the majority of my earnings to my family overseas.

My mom immigrated to the US when I was born and has a major gambling problem.

My kids live overseas with their dad and I need to make sure I save enough money to visit and host them when they come.

My adult child is dependent on me.

We won the lottery to leave Russia and moved to the US with nothing on very short notice.

Giving

I want to practice meaningful giving and get into philanthropy.

I have inherited more wealth than I can possibly spend in this lifetime. I need to integrate my new reality and be a good steward of this gift.

I want to provide for my daughter and grandchildren.

I am a widow with enough money to last several generations. I have ideas for several community foundations, but more than anything, I didn't want to be alone with my wealth.

Health and Aging

I'm losing sleep.

I am a creative/type B personality and I need to improve my relationship with money.

I have ADD and I'm a disaster with money.

I'm sixty-five years old and haven't saved for retirement.

I'm sixty-nine years old and never learned how to balance a checkbook. I need to start paying attention.

We want to retire, but don't have enough saved up.

I played in the NFL and suffered so many concussions, I am now on disability.

Planning

I just received an inheritance and have $500,000 in my checking account. I have no idea what to do now.

We bought a house and need a budget.

My kids are going to college and I want to downsize.

I'm twenty-eight years old and still relying on my parents. I want to get things under control and be independent.

We want to transition to full feral [homesteading] in the next three to five years."

I want to get out of survival mode.

Debt Management

I need help creating a strategic debt repayment plan.

I am sick of the credit card debt cycle.

I have mounting debt and I cannot see beyond it.

After my parents spent my college savings on themselves, I took out loan after loan and now have $340,000 in student debt.

Financial Trauma

My lifestyle changed from having a complete household staff at my beck and call to living alone in a tiny apartment with $155,000 of credit card debt. I am spiraling out of control.

I grew up with generational wealth, but a series of bad decisions as well as being numb and terrified have led me to personal bankruptcy.

I grew up very poor. We had a tin roof, no electricity, and no plumbing. I used to sleep with bricks, warmed by the sun, to keep from freezing at night.

I have a serious aversion to taking care of my financial life.

I grew up with massive wealth and it's all gone.

I grew up surrounded by abuse and addiction. I was emancipated at sixteen, but my parents assumed credit cards in my name and maxed them out. All of the accounts ended up in collections and it ruined my credit.

We lost everything in a bank robbery in Haiti. Years of hard work disappeared.

I filed for bankruptcy ten years ago and my habits never changed.

General Help

I've never been good with money.

I am cash flow negative.

I want to be more deliberate and intentional with my money.

I want to join the FIRE [Financial Independence, Retire Early] movement.

I need an accurate picture of my finances.

I need a basic personal finance education and skill set.

I want to give my money purpose.

My inheritance was much larger and more complicated than I ever imagined.

I need accountability.

I need to overcome my lifelong dysfunction with money.

I want my personal finances to flow like a well-oiled machine.

I've been completely avoidant and unconscious about money until now.

I'm on a path to elevate my integrity with money.

I need to change my relationship with money.

I am reassessing my financial life and have a lot to learn.

Financial Psychology Research

Financial education, which can be acquired formally through high school and college classes, personal finance seminars, or informally through the mentoring of family members, friends, or employers, can have a significant impact on financial outcomes.

Money coaching clients are everyday people like you and me. I've worked with parents, horse trainers, professional athletes, actors, musicians, supermodels, publishers, nannies, general contractors, stay-at-home moms, stay-at-home dads, lawyers, doctors, teachers, professors, students, musicians, environmental activists, executive assistants, nutritionists, producers, law enforcement officers, firefighters, personal assistants, unemployed folks, financial advisors, administrators, dancers, playwrights, oil heiresses, empty nesters, medical experts, millennials, coaches, project managers, entrepreneurs, realtors, psychotherapists, DJs, midwives, doulas, adult children of C-suite tech giants, artists, architects, news anchors, students, tattoo artists, authors, lawyers, influencers, bodyworkers, shop keepers, sex workers, nonprofit and corporate executives, estheticians, personal trainers, parent coaches, dog walkers, pediatric neurologists, writers, officers in the military, postal workers, producers, novelists, stagehands, social workers, interior designers, people navigating inherited wealth, and others integrating earned wealth. This list is only a sample of my real money coaching clients and not intended to exclude anyone. All are welcome here!

Chapter One
Tracking

How to Relax About Money

Money is a naturally confronting topic, so we need to take extra loving care of ourselves when dealing with it. There are numerous simple, yet powerful breathing and bodywork exercises you can do right now or anytime you need to manage feelings and reduce anxiety. You have the control to increase a feeling of calm and expand your sense of connection to the Universe at your fingertips. When you're centered and grounded, your money and communication will flow more easily. You're more likely to respond than react. Breathing exercises can bring you out of scarcity and fear, back into your body and the present moment. The hardest part is recognizing when you're dysregulated and then remembering to employ a tool.

Each one of these techniques is designed to help you pause, slow down, clear your mind, decrease your heart rate, strengthen your concentration, soften your grip, and let go of any sense of urgency. Try one exercise at a time, or one every day. Easy does it. If you have the luxury of time, begin and end each stress-reducing exercise with a few deep breaths in through your nose and out through your mouth. Give your brain a chance to change the channel and reset. Let's harness the power of *pranayama*, the ancient practice of breath control.

Relaxation and Feelings Management Exercises

- Place the tip of the tongue against the roof of your mouth.
- Alternate nostril breathing.
- Squeeze your thumb and first finger between your thumb and first finger of one hand, then switch.
- Inhale for three seconds, then exhale for five seconds.
- Place your hand in front of your mouth to feel the warm and cool breaths.
- Wiggle your toes.
- Practice mindful walking, where you focus on feeling the floor or ground beneath your feet.
- Spend time in nature. Go outside and face the sun or walk around the block.
- Place two fingers on your lips and hold.
- Scan your body head to toe with breath awareness.
- Clench your fists and let go.
- Lie on your back with one hand on your belly, with the other hand on your chest. Notice your hands moving up and down with each breath.

- Rub your eyes very gently and soften your gaze, taking everything in. Then, harden your gaze by focusing intently on one object.
- Place open hands palms down on your belly just under your rib cage. Notice the distance between your thumbs goes closer and farther apart with each breath.
- Practice contemplative prayer/meditation.
- Try restorative or yin yoga.
- Try a Thai massage (or any style of bodywork).

Write down three techniques you're willing to try:

1.
2.
3.

The How to Relax About Money exercise can be found at sfmoneycoach.com/downloads.

Some of these techniques can be as short as a few seconds, and others can be repeated for several minutes. Your favorites may shift over time. You can use sensory experiences like these before, during, or after emotionally challenging financial moments. One-minute meditations are also useful for managing the mess of everyday life. Tap into your parasympathetic nervous system when you need to bring an overwhelming sensation or thought back to its right size. Remember, this too shall pass.

Values Clarification

Now that you're relaxed, we can go a little deeper and explore your core values. In Seattle, Washington, I attended a four-day women's wealth weekend called "The Awakening." I was very much in a "go-go-go" phase of my life, and definitely focused on doing over being. Barbara Huson, the renowned leader, could apparently sense the pain in my heart. She called me out and asked me to stand up in front of the group for some one-on-one feedback. I lamented about how hard I'd worked on myself and whined about how much effort was involved with adulting. I described how utterly torturous it was—privately and publicly—that I didn't have the guy, the house, or the children I so deeply desired. Basically everything I ever worried about in my life, including money, came down to this unrequited dream.

She yelled, "Stop it!" The room seized up. "Carrie, you need to sit on your hands more and do *nothing* for a while. You're addicted to *busy*-ness!" She was right. My ego (edging God out) was a bit bruised, but I liked, trusted, and respected her immensely. I tried to mine the gold and received the feedback as gracefully as I could. And I stayed present. The old me would have huffed and puffed back in my seat. Instead, I remained open and listened when she moved on and recommended the following values clarification exercise to the group.

Problem is, many of us haven't a clue what we value most in life. And then we wonder what's missing. I learned how important it is to identify and prioritize my values when I interviewed seven-figure women. The ones who were most satisfied with their lives and had the most balance, while making good money, actually took the time to prioritize their values, and make decisions accordingly. Reprinted with permission from Barbara Stanny Huson's *Overcoming Underearning.*

Circle the ten values that are most important to you. If you don't see an important value on this list, add it. Give yourself time to really explore and think about these.

achievement	freedom	justice	self-esteem
acceptance	friendship	kindness	self-discipline
adventure	fun	knowledge	service
aging well	generosity	leadership	simplicity
beauty	God	learning	spirituality
brother/sisterhood	growth	leaving a legacy	strength
charity	happiness	leisure	success
comfort	harmony	life partner	support
community	health	love	surrender
commitment	honesty	making a difference	time alone
communication	honor	parenting	transformation
courage	humility	patriotism	travel
creativity	independence	peace	truth
democracy	individuality	physical activity	using my talents
dignity	influence	power	wisdom
discovery	inner peace	respect	others
diversity	integrity	responsibility	fitness
education	intimacy	retirement	
family	joy	security	

Cross out five words that you've circled and rank the remaining five in order of importance.

My most important values are:

1.
2.
3.
4.
5.

Now that you know what values are most important to you, from this point on, before saying *yes* or *no* to anything, ask yourself this question: Will this bring me closer to, or take me farther away from, living in alignment with my values?

The Values Clarification exercise can be found at sfmoneycoach.com/downloads.

Personal Finance Goals

Once you've clarified your core values, you can then access the layer of insight and intuition where your goals are. The Universe and your money are listening. Use positive language. For example, instead of, "I do not want to feel stuck in my career," say, "I am earning a promotion at work," or, "I feel happy, confident, and inspired at work." Contemplate the essential areas of your relationship with money: spending, saving, and earning. You might also consider relationships, family history, giving, aging and health, planning, debt management, financial trauma, and general help. Include how you want to feel emotionally, spiritually, and psychologically about money plus anything else that comes to mind. Here are some questions to consider.

1. What's at stake for you in your financial life?
2. What do you want to address and accomplish in the next three to six months?
3. How do you want your relationship with money to change in the next one to two years?
4. Three to five years?
5. Longterm?

Write down your goals. Trust your gut on this. You can always edit them later. If you need inspiration, check out some common personal finance goals from my actual clients below.

Spending: I Want To…

- Know where my money is going
- Buy a house
- Reduce overall spending
- Identify and stop leaks in spending
- Address patterns of overspending
- Experience guilt-free, no-harm spending
- Be free from compulsive spending

Saving: I Want To…

- Build and sustain multiple levels of savings at once
- Figure out my savings goals for periodic expenses, safety net, kids' college tuition, travel, taxes, large purchases, and so forth
- Know when I can retire

Earning: I Want To…

- Overcome a pattern of underearning

- Manifest satisfying work
- Earn at least $_______ per year
- Create a business plan
- Change jobs
- Develop multiple streams of passive income

Relationships: I Want To…

- Feel comfortable talking to _______ about money
- Experience a solid financial partnership with _______
- Financially prepare for divorce
- Stop prioritizing other people's needs over my own

Emotions: I Want To…

- Have more clarity and intention around money
- Have a sense of control
- Feel secure, confident, and savvy, while experiencing a sense of abundance with money
- Feel empowered and competent with money
- Feel light, be clear, and experience flow around money
- Express my freedom, gratitude, and joy with money
- Reduce anxiety and stress about money
- Let go of avoidance and scarcity thinking
- Identify and overcome limiting beliefs
- Fully understand and integrate my inherited wealth including my feelings, questions, and hopes

Family: I Want To…

- Provide grounded financial modeling for _______
- Wean my adult child off financial support
- Make clear agreements with _______

Planning: I Want To…

- Create a household budget and spending plan
- Maintain a comfortable cushion in my checking accounts of at least $_______ in personal and $_______in business at all times
- Plan a renovation
- Plan for a comfortable retirement
- Gracefully prepare for my inheritance
- Stay in my current home
- Plan my wedding and honeymoon
- Live within my means
- Stop giving away my time for free
- Be solvent

Health and Aging: I Want To…

- Prepare for financial agency in my elderly parents' lives
- Retire as early as possible
- Understand our finances better in case I lose my husband to his degenerative disease

Giving: I Want To…

- Practice no-harm giving
- Be generous and of service to people and institutions I care about
- Get into philanthropy

Debt Management: I Want To…

- Eliminate all consumer debt and prevent future debt
- Increase my credit score

General Help: I Want To…

- Simplify and streamline my financial life
- Level up my relationship with money
- Develop self-accountability
- Increase self-awareness in the house of money
- Enjoy balance and alignment with my finances
- Have a system for spending, saving, earning, and investing with mindfulness
- Practice conscious financial decision-making
- Develop sustainable personal finance routines
- Learn the ABCs and 123s of personal finance

Now that we have set the stage with relaxation techniques and your goals, you're ready to start tracking—that is, knowing where your money is going. The word *sati*, in the context of Buddhism, means mindfulness, or being aware of what is. Tracking requires being totally present with your cash flow. Taking the advice of my money coach, I literally wrote down every single transaction I made or that hit my account, by hand, in a checkbook register. Believe me, I was resistant, even appalled by the suggestion at first. I tried it anyway since I was paying her after all and hated wasting money. The process turned out to be very educational and empowering. For the first time in my life, I understood money. Like an anthropologist, I studied the ins and outs of my own checking account, and it was enlightening. Today, it is almost unheard of to take an extra five seconds at a store checkout counter or pause before exiting a taxi to write down how much you spent by hand. But, if this exercise calls to you, trust your intuition. Think of it as a daily wheatgrass shot or push-ups. It could be really good for you!

The goal of tracking is to remain curious and pay attention to your money. Trust me, *your money will speak to you*. What you focus on expands. And tracking your money for just thirty days can change your life. Thanks to your brain's innate plasticity, new habits can literally rewire your thinking and reactions, even in adults. Ninety days of tracking is even more powerful and sets the foundation for creating a healthy and sustainable relationship with money. Technology and modern life have changed so much since then, and I will share all kinds of efficient options with you. In Buddhism, the word *samadhi* is commonly used to describe mental discipline and concentration, , and both will be required.

How to Balance a Checkbook

In case you're like me and no one ever sat down with you to demonstrate the basic life skill of tracking your finances, we can practice together now.

1. Choose a modality. Where do you like taking notes? This could be a small notebook, a classic checkbook register, or an app. If you go old-school with a checkbook register, you can pick one up for free at any bank. And you might consider decorating the cover. I added sparkly heart stickers and affirmations printed in purple calligraphy to mine in an attempt to feel good and eventually find pleasure in picking up the damn thing. Which option makes you feel happy, joyous, and free? Some apps I have explored are Google Sheets, iPhone Notes, Checkbook, and Expense Manager. We will

explore comprehensive personal finance software programs in the next chapter.

2. Set up your tracking system with separate registers for each of your accounts. At the very least, track your primary checking account, any active credit cards, and your cash. If you're using a notebook, each account should be tracked on a separate page. In a checkbook register, use paper clips to easily separate your accounts. On Google Sheets, use separate tabs for each.
3. The current balance is the first transaction in each register. For your cash, count your money and record that amount. For checking and credit card accounts, log in online and record the balance. Don't include pending transactions. You will capture those when they post.
4. Now you can start tracking! Out and about in your daily life, record every single thing that happens to your money: debit card purchases, deposits, checks, credit card charges, bills, ATM withdrawals, bill payments, paychecks, and quick-pay transactions like Venmo, PayPal, and Zelle. You will need to log in to online banking more frequently to make sure you don't miss anything that may usually go unseen like reimbursements, automatic payments, or refunds. Transfers will affect two of your registers. For example, when withdrawing cash from the ATM, you will subtract the amount from your checking register and add the amount to your cash register. The same mechanics apply to credit card payments. Record the transfer of funds in both registers—where the money came from and where it went.

5. Do the math. Practice the courage to subtract. Every day, use a big-button calculator to subtract what you spent and add what you deposited. Maintain a running balance in each register. Some people prefer to collect receipts instead of recording transactions on the go. I suggest getting current in your registers as soon as you get home so you can toss the receipts. Don't let them pile up or they will grow hair and fangs. If you miss a day or a series of transactions, don't stop tracking. Simply correct the balance and move on!

Here's an example of a pristine checkbook:

DATE	WHO/WHAT/WHERE	OUT	IN	BALANCE
1/9	starting balance			$2,389.11
1/9	groceries	$121.06		
1/9	paycheck		$2,560	$4,828.05
1/10	coffee	$7.03		
1/10	H&M	$270.28		
1/10	car payment	$375.46		
1/10	ATM	$120		
1/10	Visa payment	$597.33		$3,457.95

Now that you've learned the bedrock of personal finance, tracking, we'll pause on the practical skills related to dollars and cents and explore the ever more nuanced psychological side of money.

Learning Styles + Money

I took a yoga class once, and the instructor gave me specific verbal instructions to deepen a pose. I saw her mouth moving and heard the words, but I could not comprehend what she was saying. She might as well have been speaking in a foreign language. "Would you show me?" I asked. She demonstrated the adjustment while repeating the instructions and it was like drinking a long, cold sip of water. I'm a visual learner.

Before becoming a money coach, I was a first grade head teacher at a progressive private school. Over the course of that nine-year career, I studied and practiced Howard Gardner's theory of multiple intelligences (MI). My personal pedagogy also included reflective teaching and positive discipline along with an equal emphasis on social emotional learning (SEL) and academics. So, what does this have to do with money? *Everything.*

To succeed in managing your cash flow, we need to tune in to what comes naturally and easily to you. New healthy habits will be more sustainable if we leverage your natural gifts and learning styles. The MI theory asserts that there are eight different intelligences, or ways of being smart:

Musical
Spatial
Linguistic
Logical—Mathematical
Bodily—Kinesthetic
Interpersonal
Intrapersonal
Naturalist

As a practitioner, it's critical for me to be self-aware so I can balance my strengths, avoid overfunctioning, and improve my weaknesses too. My coaching and presentation style needs to remain adaptable for more than one type of learning or processing style. When I completed the MI assessment, the results suggested my three strongest intelligences were spatial, bodily—kinesthetic, and musical. It made so much sense and felt like, "Yep, that's me!" I love art and color and I'm extremely sensitive to my physical surroundings, which manifests in a constant need for organization (control) and visual order. I am someone who enjoys cleaning and tidying. I've been playing competitive sports consistently for four decades—particularly tennis and, more recently, pickleball too. The court is my joy location. Musically, I am a beginner at ten different instruments and love to sing and dance. I am always listening to music and have a modest entertainment budget for live music as well. Some of my all-time favorite concerts include the Grateful Dead, U2, Beyonce, Aimee Mann, and Imogen Heap. For as long as I can remember, I have been playing music to enhance my moods, express my feelings and process life's ups and downs. My clients embody all eight learning styles, so I try my best to be flexible and customize our conversations, their financial-wellness activities, and their homework, accordingly. Here are some tried-and-true ways in which all kinds of minds can feel successful with money.

<u>Musical—Rhythmic</u>: Play your favorite rhythmic or harmonic music while you're looking at or talking about money. You know that particular song or album that makes you happy, no matter what? When you turn the music on, notice any changes in your attitude, willingness, or perspective. Create a playlist of upbeat money songs or try composing one.

Visual—Spatial: Decorate your checkbook cover or buy a new wallet. Create a vision board on Pinterest or, better yet, go old-school and gather inspiring images from magazines to make a collage of your best life. Organize your desk area and add flowers, a candle, and your favorite pens. A large computer monitor can also spark the flow. Draw a map of how money flows through your various accounts. Create a poster or comic strip of your history with money. Generate some colorful charts, graphs, and tables representing your spending, saving, and earning.

Verbal—Linguistic: Listen to a money podcast while you're doing financial housekeeping work. Read an article about personal finance before, during (if you need a break), and after a money date. Debrief what you learned with a friend or family member. Keep a journal to articulate your thoughts, feelings, and questions about money. Write a letter to the editor of a newspaper or an op-ed piece about what it means to have a relationship with money.

Logical—Mathematical: Think of your spending plan like a puzzle and try to problem solve when you face a shortfall. Calculate your total spending, saving, and earning for the month and for the year. Keep your balances updated and accurate for all of your accounts in a tracking app, spreadsheet, software program, or small notebook. Choose an overall personal bookkeeping system that provides you with peace of mind, confidence, and a sense of control. Create a timeline of your life's journey with money, for example, earning levels, spending habits, debt, savings, and investments.

Bodily—Kinesthetic: Use a standing desk or another high counter for your computer, notes, and papers while you're working on your finances. Wear comfortable clothes and take stretch breaks when needed. Keep your favorite supplies nearby and organized. Some of my personal favorites are pens, a nice notebook, calculator, ice water, cozy blanket, and essential oils. Create a human tableau of your happiest and most painful memories with money. Describe what happened through interpretive dance. Role-play a variety of characters with money (e.g., a sibling, celebrity, money manager model, or parent).

Interpersonal: Have dates with your best financial friend (BFF) or partner and articulate your financial reality. Work on your money at a café surrounded by people. Join a money meetup, personal finance club, or investment group. Survey positive financial role models in your life. Interview your parents about their individual relationships with money.

Intrapersonal: Turn your phone off. Go to any lengths to be alone with your money. Choose a place where you can take time for reflection. Self-monitor your effort and activity in your financial life. Listen to your inner voice and intuition. Document major financial events in a journal or log. Share your experiences with and opinions about money in a speech or editorial.

Naturalist: Open a window and take deep breaths. Listen to a soothing audio track of nature sounds. Sit outside or indoors near a plant and in bright natural light when focusing on your money. Look for patterns in your spending and saving habits. Write a brochure about a major financial event as though traveling to another country. Classify and display foreign coins and bills. Connect with positive financial role models and invest in these relationships.

I highly recommend experimenting with some of these ideas in your personal money practice. Making minor adjustments to your space, style, or process can make all the difference in feeling more relaxed and happier about money. You can pick and choose what inspires you on any given day!

Tune in and write down three of these suggestions that conjure hope or feel inspiring:

1.
2.
3.

Exercises for Self-Awareness

"This above all: to thine own self be true."
—Act I, Scene III of *Hamlet*
by William Shakespeare

I encourage you to increase your *intrapersonal intelligence*, a.k.a. self-awareness. That is, the ability to connect and check in withyourself. This insight is critical to seeing if your thoughts and behaviors are aligned with your highest self. The more self-aware you are, the more choices you will have in your financial life. For example, if you know you're vulnerable to overspending late at night on your phone, self-awareness can help you recognize when you're triggered or when a slip has occurred and potentially curb the amount you spend or even prevent you from going down that rabbit hole at all. Self-awareness is critical to knowing when you're dysregulated and might need to take a break for some mindful breathing. Pausing creates space between your thoughts and actions and is one of the most powerful tools in personal finance.

I remember a time when I was shopping in a boutique on Fillmore Street in Pacific Heights. I must have just come from a money date because I literally sat down on the bench in the dressing room and pulled out the calculator on my phone. I looked at each price tag from the pile of clothes I wanted and added them up. I rounded up a bit for tax and took a moment to digest the grand total. What was even more shocking was that I ended up buying only half of the items. Without self-awareness, overspending would have been inevitable that day. There are innumerable ways to explore the emotional, spiritual, and psychological sides of money. Here are some readily accessible tools for expanding your self-awareness:

- Multiple Intelligences for Adults and Strengths Survey http://www.literacynet.org/mi/assessment/findyourstrengths.html
- Character and Strengths Survey https://viacharacter.org/survey/account/register
- Money Script Inventory-Revised (KSMI-R) https://wwwbradklontz.com.moneyscripttest
- Money Behavior Inventory (KMBI) https://bradklontz.com/moneybehaviortest
- Financial Health Scale (FHS) https://www.bradklontz.com/financialhealthtest
- Personality Assessor https://www.personalityassessor.com/bigfive/
- Love, Apology, Anger, and Appreciation Language Quizzes https://5lovelanguages.com/quizzes

Links for the Self-Awareness Exercises can be found at sfmoneycoach.com/resources.

"The unexamined life is not worth living,"—a quote attributed to the ancient Greek philosopher Socrates—carries a profound meaning that invites us to examine our own existence and choices. Socrates believed that a life devoid of introspection, self-reflection, and critical thinking is essentially meaningless and lacks value. This quote emphasizes the importance of self-awareness and questioning one's beliefs, actions, internal standards, and purpose in life.

Personal Capital, a.k.a. Net Worth

It turns out that money is just one aspect of your net worth. Traditional net worth is defined by assets minus liabilities. Personal assets have economic value and can include cash, investments, retirement accounts, property (home or land), vehicles, personal belongings, and life insurance policies plus gold and silver. According to the Investopedia team, business assets can include motor vehicles, buildings, machinery, equipment, cash, and accounts receivable, as well as intangibles like patents, intellectual property, royalties, and trademarks. Liabilities are just the opposite: something that is owed to another person, company, or the governmenttypically a loan, debt, outstanding bill, or tax obligation.

To be financially healthy, you must have access to and understand your numeric net worth. I suggest that you obtain and record the balances of all assets and liabilities once a quarter, that is, at least four times a year. And, if you're married or in a committed partnership, you will need three columns for Mine,

Yours, and Ours. The grand total number itself is finite. Your personal capital provides a more holistic, expansive infinite view of your net worth including strengths, skills, relationships, and noneconomic materials. The self-awareness exercises above may help to shed light as you ponder your personal capital.

What did you learn about your own money-related behavior and thought patterns?

____

____

____

____

____

List your top strengths.

____

____

____

____

____

List your skills (e.g., areas of competency and mastery).

____

____

____

____

____

List your primary relationships (e.g. family, professional connections, and friends).

____

List your favorite noneconomic materials in unlimited supply (e.g., sunsets, mountains, and laughter).

The first time I did this exercise, it was an emotional turning point. I hope that, even if you have a negative net worth like I did at the time, for just a moment, you're able to bask in the amazing abundance in your life. You are *so much more* than your money.

You can download the Personal Capital Exercise at sfmoneycoach.com/downloads.

Life-Energy Number

So far, we have covered how to relax about money, values, goals, tracking, learning styles, the concept and responsibility of self-awareness, and personal capital. Now, let's talk about how much things *actually* cost in terms of time and energy. This calculation will shed light on future purchases, whether it's a major money event like seasonal clothes shopping, traveling, buying property, or planning a wedding or a minor decision like going out for coffee, taking a taxi, or renewing a streaming service.

1. Let's assume you make a salary of $75,000 a year. That is your gross income. But as you have likely noticed, you don't get to keep all of that. So, what is your net income? After taxes and deductions, what amount gets deposited into your account? Let's say your net earning is $5,000 a month.
2. What other costs are associated with making that money? Do you have to maintain an expensive wardrobe or drive a nice car? Do you have to eat out for lunch a lot? Are you so tired at the end of the day that you order in more than you would like? Let's say all of those costs add up to an extra $600/month. So really, your "net earning" of truly available money is $4,400 ($5,000 – $600 = $4,400). Still with me?
3. How many hours did you *really* have to work for this $4,400? If you're salaried, add up all your hours. I vote that you throw in your commute time as well. You wouldn't be spending those forty-five minutes commuting if you didn't need to work for money, right? Some people even like to include the time they need to get ready in the morning. Let's assume that you add up the time you commute and the hours you are at work and it equals fifty-five hours.
4. Take fifty-five hours and multiply by four weeks per month (55 × 4 = 220 hours each month). Technically, there are 4.2 weeks in a month, for those of you who are into being

> exact. Let's say you've spent 220 hours to earn that $4,400. Now, divide your true take-home pay by the amount of life energy you had to expend to get it ($4,400 divided by 220 hours is 20). Twenty is your Life-Energy Number.

If this was my Life-Energy Number, here's how I would use it. Let's say I'm in Nordstrom eyeing a pair of one-hundred-dollar shoes. I'd simply ask myself, *Are those shoes worth five hours of my life energy?*

If I'm contemplating an $800 weekend getaway to Lake Tahoe, I may ask myself, *Is this trip worth forty hours of my life energy*?

Or perhaps, when I'm out shopping for holiday gifts, I can ask myself, *Are these gifts, totaling $400, for my nine nieces and nephews worth twenty hours of my life energy?*

Sometimes the answer is *yes*, and sometimes it is *no*. This fundamental knowledge and insight into your time, energy and money puts a wonderfully different spin on things. Knowing your Life-Energy Number serves as a bookmark. Pausing to reflect on your number will ideally lead to more no-harm, guilt-free shopping experiences.

Explore the official Life-Energy Calculator at yourmoneyoryourlife.com/life-energy-calculator. Adapted from Vicki Robinsand Joe Dominguez's *Your Money or Your Life*.

Messy-Wallet People

A word to messy-wallet people. Are you one of those people who still carries a wallet and unnecessarily stuffs it with filmy receipts and other loot? Do you capture or file the receipts and remove them from your wallet in a timely manner? Do you carry more plastic than you need to for everyday life, like frequent-flier cards or specific store credit cards? Contrary to what you might think, this kind of clutter can increase money fog and magical thinking. If you're a longtime messy-wallet person, chances are that the finance department is not the only area in your life where you are procrastinating or cluttering. Ideally, you want your wallet to be beautiful yet functional, minimalistic, and fitting for your personality and style. Most importantly, your wallet should support your money flow.

One day, I was shopping in Union Square in San Francisco—a rare treat. I had known for a while that it was time to let go of my colorful hippie change pouch and buy a new, grown-up wallet. I walked into Kate Spade, which I still consider high-end, and spent over $200 on a gorgeous gold-colored, checkbook-size wallet with a hot pink leather interior. This was totally extravagant for me but also a game changer. I immediately started experiencing more feelings of joy, pride, and abundance every time I touched the wallet. I give you permission to upgrade too!

Ideas for elevating your wallet game:

- Buy a new wallet—highly recommended!
- Clean out your wallet at least once a week.
- Remove credit cards you don't need or want to use.
- Create a digital wallet.
- Stop carrying change.
- Buy a cell phone cover that doubles as a wallet.

The bottom line is that how we take care of our money is how we take care of ourselves, our relationships, and the world. *How you do money is how you do life.*

Chapter Two
Planning

Once you start gathering accurate numbers about your current lifestyle via tracking, it's time to use the data to advance your relationship with money. No one has a crystal ball and knows *exactly* what will happen in the upcoming month, but the practice of creating a spending plan, a.k.a. budget, gives you the opportunity to be intentional and stay connected. This monthly routine is not only grounding, but a preventive measure against money fog, magical thinking, and overspending.

You Need a System

We already discussed simple cash flow tracking, but with inherent limits, these tools will only take you so far. The number one best thing you can do for your relationship with money is to choose a SYSTEM, to Save Yourself Time, Energy, and

Money, through comprehensive personal finance or bookkeeping software.

It can be challenging to get started since there is a plethora of apps, programs, and websites to choose from. As of 2025, my favorite financial tracking software program is Quicken for Mac. Do your own research and consider checking out other awesome programs like YNAB, Rocket Money, Monarch Money, Google's Tiller, QuickBooks, and MoneyGrit. I highly recommend the FinTech (financial technology) route for long-term sustainability, but I want to be truthful with you. In my experience, you may need to spend five to ten *hours* on setup, practice, and learning the new system—not five to ten *minutes* like they all advertise. Don't panic, I promise the commitment is worthwhile. Whichever system you choose, make sure categories can be customized according to your vocabulary and values, that budgeting is available by month and by year, and robust customer service can be very useful in getting through the learning curve.

Values-Based Categories

So how do you start budgeting? After you have purchased or created a system that works for you, the next step is to decide how many categories you need. I'm not exaggerating to say that I used to use fifty categories to track my money. When I started my financial wellness journey, I literally needed to know that I had exactly $20 for the movies, $350 for groceries, and $35 for taxis. Over the course of tracking my spending for two decades, I have shifted my approach and philosophy about categories. Today, I require less detail in my budget to remain solvent;

therefore, my category buckets are much larger. I have narrowed my category list down to just sixteen:

Home
Food
Clothes
Health Care
Self-Care
Kids
Transportation
Entertainment
Sports
Travel
Gifts
Taxes
Insurance
Professional Development
Savings
Debt Repayment (if needed)

I still utilize specific subcategories for Travel and Income. I use actual destinations as catch-all subcategories for my adventures so I can budget and plan for trips and be able to see the total actual cost of each trip in one place.

Travel
Florida
Mendocino
Fallen Leaf Lake
Income
Coaching
Courses

Partner Paycheck
Tax Refund
Rental Income

Under Income, it is super important to establish subcategories for *all possible streams of inflow* in a given year. With clarity on income projections, you can plan accordingly, understand how much you need to work and earn, and anticipate your monthly and annual spending limits.

If you're just beginning the budgeting journey, a larger number of categories may be useful for clearing the money fog and helping you to remain in the green. You may intuitively know you have hot-spot areas of spending and need a higher level of awareness and accountability in that area. And, the more subcategories you use, the more time and energy it will take to plan and track your spending. Check out this comprehensive list of main categories and subcategories:

INCOME

Salary 1
Salary 2
Bonus 1
Bonus 2
Stock or Other Sale
Gifts
Tax Refund
Rental Income
Reimbursements

EXPENSES	
HOME	Rent/Mortgage
	Homeowner Dues
	Property Taxes
	Homeowner's Insurance
	Household Supplies
	Cable/Internet
	Cell Phone
	Water
	Garbage
	Electricity/Gas
	Security System
	Maintenance/Repairs
	Improvement Projects
	Furniture/Decorations
	Gardening
	Cleaning Service
	Plants/Flowers
	Storage
FOOD	Groceries
	Meals Out/Delivery
	Coffee Shops
SPIRITUAL/PERSONAL GROWTH	Classes
	Retreats
CLOTHES	Wardrobe 1
	Wardrobe 2
	Dry Cleaning

HEALTH CARE	Health Insurance
	Pharmacy/Vitamins
	Doctor
	Dentist
	Optical
	Therapy
	Nutritionist
	Bodywork
SELF-CARE	Hair
	Health Club
	Exercise Classes
	Nails/Beauty Treatments
	Skin Care
TRANSPORTATION	Car Payment
	Gas
	Car Insurance
	Registration
	Maintenance/Repairs
	Tolls
	Parking
	Car Wash
	Rideshare
	Public Transportation
ENTERTAINMENT	Subscriptions
	iTunes/Google Play
	Books/Magazines
	Tickets
	Date Nights
	Hobbies

	Parties
	Holiday Decorations
KIDS	Childcare
	Supplies
	Gear
	Clothes
	Classes/Sports
	Toys/Books
	Entertainment/Tickets
PETS	Food/Supplies
	Vet
	Gear
TRAVEL	Trip 1
	Trip 2
	Trip 3
HOLIDAYS/GIFTS	Seasonal Holidays
	Birthdays
	Weddings/Showers
	Misc.
HOME OFFICE	Computer/Phone Stuff
	Office Supplies
	Renewals
	Accountant
	Attorney
	Money Coach
	Financial Planner

TAXES	IRS/Federal
	State
	City
EDUCATION/PROFESSIONAL DEVELOPMENT	Licenses/Certifications
	Tuition
	Supplies/Books
	Classes
INSURANCE	Life
	Disability
	Long-Term Care
	Other
DEBT REPAYMENT	School Loan
	Line of Credit
	Personal Loan
	Back Taxes
	Credit Card 1
	Credit Card 2

You can find the link to Sample Budget Categories at sfmoneycoach.com/downloads.

Spending Plans, a.k.a. Budgets

Once your categories are set for the upcoming year, then you're ready to create your first spending plan. Wahoo! For now, focus only on the upcoming month. Record your planned and intended spending, saving, and earning for the month. Line by line, category by category. Envision the envelope system—back in the day before credit became a form of currency, people would cash their paychecks and literally sort their available cash into labeled envelopes (e.g., "Bills" and "Groceries"). They would then use the allotted funds until the money ran out, and that was it. There was flexibility such that you could move money out of one envelope to another, but there was still a limited amount of cash available. Spending plans, a.k.a budgets, follow the same methodology, but modern life, credit, and technology have made the process more complicated. The first budget is always the hardest one to complete since you may need to locate files, look things up or request information. Remember, it's okay to estimate or guess in the beginning. You need to start somewhere; just drop a pin for now. Trust that every month, your spending plans will become more and more accurate; that's inevitable. Pause with each category and ask yourself, *What's honest and what's realistic?*

There are three levels of spending plans: bare-bones, middle-of-the-road, and lifestyle-of-your-dreams. If you're living paycheck to paycheck, a bare-bones spending plan is the place to start. Go through the process of taking a careful look at the income picture and naming a number for every spending category ensuring basic needs are met: food, shelter, clothing, bills, and safety. A hard, sober look can feel uncomfortable, and you may be a little shaky at first. And, being in reality will ultimately boost your self-esteem and confidence while providing some relief. It's worth it and you're worth it.

In my coaching practice, many individuals, even high earners, come to their first appointment stressed and barely scraping by. The money fog is often thick and at the end of every month, they wonder where their money went. They run their accounts very lean and rely on credit cards to make ends meet.

Financial Psychology Research
Financial stress is associated with the inability to meet one's economic responsibilities.

There are many dangers in excessive credit card use—*false income.* Like it or not, the balance owed will eventually catch up with you. You must pay back every penny plus, if you carry a balance month to month, you will be dinged up to thirty percent in interest charges on each statement. Living in financial denial can cause regret, remorse, shame, and hopelessness not to mention the psychic pain of drowning and feeling stuck. Sadly, people often cope with consumer debt by spending more to get that dopamine release (relief), prompting the cycle to start all over again.

Middle-of-the-road spending plans address the whole financial picture including the past, present, and future. Folks creating these plans already know their liability picture in detail, and there is a modicum of stability, consistency, and accountability built into their budget. Fear, scarcity, and worry have been replaced with financial and emotional security. Basic needs are covered, non-monthly expenses are anticipated, and there is some flexibility for spontaneity and pleasure. Now, your money is working for you!

Most of us, including myself, are not celebrities, ultrawealthy, living on trust funds, or earning seven figures or more. But as an eternal optimist, I love thinking about the lifestyle of my dreams. What would happen if your income doubled, tripled, or even quadrupled? My vision includes a private plane, designing, building, and furnishing a custom house, driving a powder-blue

Vespa around town, and having a personal chef specializing in organic vegetarian food. Dreams are fun, important, and invigorating to think about, and there's a time and place. When you're creating a spending plan, rather than shooting for the moon and giving in to every craving, remember your values, consider your goals, and strive for balance. A tenet of Buddhism *seekthe middle path*.

Once you've given your money purpose for the next thirty days and listed out your planned spending, saving, and earning, it's time for that fifth-grade math.

<u>INFLOW</u>
Checking Account Balance + Monthly Net Income + Transfers *from* Savings = **Total Cash In**
<u>OUTFLOW</u>
Total Planned Spending + Transfers *to* Savings = **Total Cash Out**
Total Cash In – Total Cash Out = Cash Flow

Hopefully the FinTech system you chose will do this math for you. You've got this. Keep breathing. Feel your feet on the floor. Now is a good time to remember how to relax about money from chapter one. The objective is to anticipate as much as possible and do the math proactively, while there's still time to make changes.

Four Solutions to a Shortfall

So, what can you do if the math doesn't work? Let's say you've tried all of my suggestions up to this point and you're still in the red. First of all, you're not alone. It took me six months to *right the ship* and create a balanced household budget and even longer to become solvent. Most adults I've met have overdrawn a checking account, bounced a check, carried consumer debt, or have run out of money between paychecks at least once. We have all made mistakes. In fact, shortfalls are the most common reason my clients kept their heads in the sand and avoided facing their finances for so long.

Overwhelm can happen to anyone, particularly those just getting into budgeting or people who are revisiting the practice after a hiatus or financial event. It can feel discouraging to do the math anddiscover you don't have enough money to live the way you want *and* pay for your bills. So, what can you do about it?

The four solutions to a shortfall are:

Increase income
Reduce expenses
Creative solutions
Communication

1: Increase Income

Maintaining and increasing income is clearly a priority for people who are financially stable and affluent and everyone knows that increasing income is not easy to do overnight. But, it needs to be top of mind for all adults in the family. If it has been more than two years since your last raise at work, it's time to advocate for it or give yourself a bump if you're the boss. The cost of inflation, alone, demands this. Do you have time, energy, and bandwidth for a side hustle? My clients have:

- Opened Etsy shops to sell their crafts
- Consigned an entire closet full of high-end clothes and shoes (worth thousands of dollars)
- Consulted or returned to areas of mastery, even when it required wearing an "old hat"
- Taken a continuing education (CE) class, professional development workshop, or earned a certificate for specialized training for a guaranteed pay raise
- Looked hard and deep at their employment situation and asked, *Is this line of work working for me?*

2: Reduce Expenses

The second solution to a shortfall is to reduce expenses. No one wants to hear this and many people assume budgeting is about cutting and slashing spending or drastically changing your lifestyle. That's not necessarily true unless you're in extremely deep water. Change can feel uncomfortable at times, just like a new yoga pose, but here are some ways to soften the blow. You can:

- Reduce, but not eliminate, expenses
- Delay, pause, or spread out household, family, or self-care services
- Negotiate with insurance and utility companies, institutions, and other vendors (make a list of all possibilities and try to tackle one per day)
- Identify and stop leaks in spending (e.g., take a weekend to empty a storage unit or cancel a streaming service you rarely use)

You'll come to see that spending less is a natural byproduct of tracking and planning because you've taken the time to plant the seeds of consciousness. You're more present with what's happening and which choices are in alignment and which ones aren't. Tracking is one way to build self-accountability, since you will be reviewing your transactions. All of these actions increase awareness when you're out and about in your daily life making financial decisions. You can do this!

3: Creative Solutions

Need to fix an imbalanced budget? Source creative solutions to your needs by thinking outside of the box. This could look like exchanging massages with your partner or a friend rather than paying for one at a spa. Rather than paying full price for clothes, you could create a clothing swap with friends, shop exclusively during sales, or hone your skills for thrifting. For babysitting needs, is there another family that you can create a kind of childcare co-op with and swap kids on a schedule? Sometimes, our bank accounts suffer from our own limited thinking. Do some research, tap the hive mind on social media, or ask your friends, family, neighbors, and colleagues about their creative solutions for curbing their monthly burn rate.

Here in the San Francisco Bay Area, we're quite obsessed with self-care, including all kinds of soothing bodywork, spiritual practices, and meditative experiences. We have an overabundance of alternative services and amenities at our fingertips: red light therapy, flotation tanks, chakra alignment, natural hot springs, acupuncture, coaching programs on every topic under the sun, watsu, rolfing, sound healing, and bullet-journaling workshops to name a few. Here's the question: do you need to have multiple sacred experiences each month? Is there a way to stagger or delay certain services and still take excellent care of yourself? What shifts would be more affordable and aligned with your truth? Something I am working on, in my own life, is allowing for more integration time . The more I slow down, in my daily life, to breathe and process, the more nectar I discover. In the stillness, I'm able to tap into moments of genuine connection and happiness.

4: Communication

Taking a stand is about looking out for number one: yourself! Financial wellness not only requires naming how you feel, what you need, and setting boundaries, but sometimes, you might also choose to share details of your reality with others. For example, "I'd love to, but I just can't afford that right now," is a perfectly acceptable response to financial pressure. But frankly, it's none of their business, and justification is not needed. "No, thank you" will do. No-harm spending means stopping all self-destructive behaviors including compulsive shopping, enabling, and financial aggression. Proactive communication can look like changing a bill due date, making a request, or delegating.

I have a client who's highly-educated, able-bodied adult son is 100 percent financially dependent at the age of thirty. My client is still working full-time at the age of sixty-five and has started maxing out his credit cards and withdrawing from his own limited retirement to fund his son's urban lifestyle. In situations like this, clear boundaries need to be set and maintained. Here are some guidelines for gradually turning off the tap:

- Set a date for when financial help will start being reduced or stop.
- Announce it to the dependent.
- Brainstorm other ideas for nonmonetary support.

- Develop a script for announcing the end.
- Develop a support system for keeping the plan in place, which may involve a third party like a fiduciary or trustee.
- Offer a referral for professional help.

Initial communication could sound like:

I love you, and I need to stop supporting you financially at this rate and frequency. Starting on the 1st, I will give you $____. On the 1st of next month, that will decrease to $____. This will continue until ____. There will be no other money available in between for bills or emergencies or anything else that comes up.

This is easier said than done. Behaviors take years to develop and great effort to change. There might be demands from the dependent to return to the previous arrangement. This can look like aggression, yelling, the silent treatment, or threats of being cut off. And that sucks! Remember, "No" is a complete sentence. It might feel just awful to lay down the line in the moment, but people rarely, if ever, regret saying no to their financial dependents in the long run. Anything is possible with sturdy parenting and self-care. Plus, you can't keep doing the same thing over and over again, expecting different results.

I have certainly attempted all four solutions at various points in my financial wellness journey. It felt awkward and I outside of my comfort zone. Shortfalls were embarrassing to talk about and no fun to manage, but I was determined to try something new since *my way* was not working.

Underearning? Who, Me?

Underearning is the pattern of earning below your potential or not making as much money as you want or need. Oh dear! The first time I calculated the total cost of my life and did the back-of-the-envelope math to figure out how much I would need to earn, *after taxes and other deductions*, to fund my plans, I was flabbergasted! I started thinking a lot about work and realized I could make more money per day in three hours of tutoring than in a whole day of classroom teaching. Years later, I walked a client through the same process, and she created an entirely different reality for herself. She was able to increase her hourly rate as a nanny by 30 percent and negotiated for health insurance and education benefits. If you suspect you may be underearning and believe that you deserve more, be on the lookout for these signs:

- Being in a "money fog"—not knowing where your money is going, how much you owe in debt, and exactly how much money you need to earn to live the life you want
- Avoiding asking for a raise
- Neglecting to raise fees for more than two years
- Excessive volunteering
- Underbilling
- Bartering
- Feeling resentful about work
- Carrying debt month to month
- Living with real or perceived deprivation—making do or doing without
- Failing to market yourself
- Quitting a job too soon

- Staying in a position too long
- Ignoring opportunity
- Underutilizing your skills
- Letting relationships (or lack thereof) hold you back financially
- No retirement account
- Not having a career plan
- Thinking that making more money is beyond your personal control
- Believing that outside forces control your financial future (external locus of control)
- Maintaining a conflicted relationship with money—believing in abundance but suffering scarcity thinking and repetitive negative financial behaviors
- Negative feelings toward wealthy people
- Being risk averse
- Secretly waiting to be rescued

Assessment + Writing Exercise:

1. Note the signs you've seen or experienced in your life. Mark each one "yes" or "no" and "passive" or "active" underearning.

   ____

   ____

   ____

   ____

   ____

2. List examples of underearning from your own life. Do some free writing: *What do you think was really going*

on there? Was there a specific fear, belief, or behavior in the way?

____

____

____

____

____

You can download the Underearning Assessment at sfmoneycoach.com/downloads.

How to Start a Small Business

Thinking of starting your own business? If it works out, it can be a great way to increase income! Is this going to be a solo venture, or are you looking to partner with someone or build a team? The first thing you need to do is clarify your business values and write down your goals and vision. My next piece of advice is to ensure you have significant savings, or another safety net, before taking the big leap. Some people keep their day jobs and "moonlight" while they research, grow and build. Depending on the business, it might be possible to maintain low to no overhead in the beginning. Before rushing out to rent the beautiful corner office on your favorite block, consider paying zero office rent for a while and work at coffee shops, in hotel lobbies, or at your kitchen table.

Capitalize on free marketing opportunities. Business cards require a nominal initial investment, but are still considered essential to have on hand for those chance encounters. Make the cards as clear and memorable as possible. Dare to be creative and choose a simple tagline. It's totally acceptable for the first attempts at marketing to be basic; there's no need to fall prey to analysis paralysis about colors, font, logo, or language. Maybe you start by sending out a mass email to your primary network—friends and family who already like, trust, and respect you. Let them know what you're doing now!

Attend local networking groups as a guest. Consider contacting Business Networking International (BNI), your local chamber of commerce, or even nearby community colleges and universities to see how you might be able to get in front of people. Hone your elevator pitch. You should be able to say what you do and who you work with in under thirty seconds. Build a website—even a one-page brochure site will do. In the beginning, I created my own version 1.0 website on an old Apple application called iWeb. Trust that in time, your brand and website will develop and expand—just like you will as a small-business owner.

Let's discuss paid marketing. There are pros and cons to social media. If you choose to create multiple accounts, be prepared to actively use them all and consider who your target audience is. I think you can not only get by, but succeed, with one profile on LinkedIn. But, it depends what you're selling. As of 2025, other options include a Facebook business page, Yelp, Instagram, X, TikTok, Google profile, Pinterest, and YouTube. There's no right or wrong way to go about marketing. Once, I got a long-term client by posting my business card on the community bulletin board at my local coffee shop, Buunni in Washington Heights, New York City. The cost? One latte.

Start with practice clients. Perhaps you can offer a reduced rate for a limited number of people. People love exclusivity and a great deal! In return, you'll have an opportunity to hone your skills. You can build out your systems, develop fluency, and increase confidence along the way. It's guaranteed you'll discover questions you didn't know you had and, most importantly, be okay with making mistakes. I worked with practice clients for several months before I officially opened my doors for business.

Have a business budget. You've got to have a financial plan for your idea, which doubles as a business plan, and should include start-up costs and periodic (non-monthly) expenses. I also suggest having a coffee and lunch budget so you can network, buy lunch for a mentor, and spend time with friends and colleagues asking questions, discussing your ideas, and requesting feedback.

Separate your business and personal finances from the start. Don't get overly excited about "writing things off." You have to wait to file taxes to enjoy this potential benefit. It goes without saying that it's essential to have a good bookkeeping system for tracking all of your business income and expenses. Until you hire an actual chief financial officer, *you* are the CFO and need to spend a minimum of one hour a week on your small-business finances. If you or someone you work or live with is not going to categorize your transactions on a consistent basis, then do yourself a favor and hire a reliable bookkeeper sooner rather than later.

Credit cards can be a slippery slope for small-business owners. I understand it sometimes takes money to make money, but do not spend on credit without a clear, grounded plan for paying it back within a time frame you can afford financially and emotionally.

You must be comfortable with the value of your services. Setting rates is a complex, intuitive, and internal process. No one else can tell you how much to charge; it must come from inside. Potential clients will read your face, body language, and voice—even over the phone—and be able to sense even an iota of desperation or nervousness. At the same time, you need to ensure you're not undercharging. No underearning allowed!During sales conversations, place both feet on the ground and take deep belly breaths. When I was preparing to launch SF Money Coach, my mentor, Mikelann Valterra, taught me seven reasons to feel confident charging at the top.

1. Education—This should include all degrees, credentials, certifications, professional development, and training.
2. Experience—Review your work history carefully and acknowledge in-industry and all industry-related experience.
3. Referrals—If your business is largely driven by referrals, well, that's awesome and enough said.
4. Results—Not sure if you're getting them? Ask for testimonials from some of your favorite clients. *What do you enjoy the most about working with me? What do you see as my greatest strength? How does working with me affect your life?*
5. Specialized Services—Do you have a clear niche? I'm a holistic money coach. Some people work exclusively with athletes, women, city dwellers, dads, or other specific groups of people.
6. Professionalism—You *know* if this applies to you and includes your website, cards, the way you dress, and your overall professionalism.
7. Ask for It—This is my favorite reason to charge at the top. Remember, you must be at ease with the request, inside and out. Go for it!

Wondering how much to pay yourself? I have learned that it takes most small-business owners three to five years to become sustainable and profitable, so it might take a while for that first paycheck. If you're the solo employee of the business, you'll likely be taking home about 50 percent of the gross (total) earnings. The range of the owner's draw can be 40 percent to 60 percent, but the other 50 percent is typically needed to cover taxes, business expenses, and retirement savings. There are incredible freedoms and potential upsides to being self-employed, and there are also tremendous responsibilities. Starting a small business can be all-consuming, exhilarating, and even overwhelming at times. It's not for the faint of heart. You need to have tough skin and a tolerance for failure and uncertainty. Keep an open mind about what you're capable of. You know your worth and you're ready for the big leap. Buckle up, it's a wild ride!

Finally, initiate a plan for managing taxes right away. Learn from my egregious, expensive mistakes with tax evasion. Avoiding taxes is a common pitfall for new small-business owners. You must be disciplined and put money aside into a separate savings account designated for taxes the moment income starts flowing. Talk to your CPA (accountant) about what percentage of your gross income you need to put aside. It's conservative to start with 20 percent to 30 percent. When I took a second pass at starting a tutoring business, I sent tax payments to the IRS and the state of California every single month in order to get the hang of paying taxes on my own. I realize that sounds extreme, but it's what I needed to do to learn the lesson. Most people simply pay quarterly estimated taxes due April 15, June 15, October 15, and January 15. Others save for taxes all year long to make one lump payment in April.

Taxes + All That Jazz

Tax season used to be my biggest nightmare. I think I may have suffered from chrometophobia—the fear of money. And, if not, then I definitely had TAD—taxpayer anxiety disorder.

Financial Psychology Research

Individuals often link their self-worth with their financial status, and, as a result, financial stress has been associated with negative life consequences affecting health, self-care, psychological well-being, academic functioning, and interpersonal relationships.

I remember a particularly awful tax deadline when I spent about a week straight in anguish trying to get the paperwork done. I stared at piles of crumpled receipts and a year's worth of bank statements, immobile for hours at a time. The previous year's transactions and unrealistic financial decision-making swirled around in my head. I felt paralyzed and ashamed. There was a zero percent chance I would attempt to file taxes on my own with a program like TurboTax. For me, that would probably trigger an aneurysm. I had no idea what to do, but at least I found the gumption to hire H&R Block at the last minute.

Even then, the questions on the standard tax questionnaire seemed *impossible* to answer. I felt so powerless and incapable. All I had to go on was a series of scribbled notes, a limited financial vocabulary, vague memories, expensive problems to undo, and terribly low self-esteem when it came to money. Tax prep was a multiday stress fest, and the CPA assigned to me had to do numeric mental gymnastics to make sense of my situation.

Here's what I discovered and learned while working to understand and process my dysregulation around taxes. My purpose in sharing these lists of healthy and anxiety-prone behaviors is not for you to pass judgment, but to offer support, choices, and tools for change. Patterns in behavioral finance are not universal, and every year can feel different financially and emotionally, so you may relate to some, but not all, or even both sides of the following taxpayer traits.

Healthy Taxpayers Tend To:

- Maintain a tax savings account.
- Have a sense of control, calm, and peace of mind while preparing taxes.
- Use an empowering, systematic approach to track personal and business expenses throughout the year.
- Experience a positive, easy, and affirming relationship with an accountant based on mutual trust and respect.
- Take time to reflect on what went well with money each year and what can be improved upon.
- Make necessary shifts and changes to set themselves up for success next tax season.
- Receive tax refunds, break even, or owe small, manageable amounts.

People At Risk for Taxpayer Anxiety Disorder:

- Suffer from negative behavior related to tax matters, including overspending, overeating, overworking, distraction, deprivation, isolation, dishonesty, imbalance, poor physical health, anxiety, loss of sleep, restlessness, irritability, or loss of appetite.

- Owe back taxes.
- Remain disempowered and uneducated about personal and business tax strategies, deductions, and liabilities, a.k.a. "just sign the papers."
- Use credit cards, overdraft accounts, or open lines of credit to pay taxes.
- Avoid tax-related responsibilities such as paperwork, deadlines, mail, or phone calls.
- Experience behavioral paralysis and are unable to address tax problems in a timely manner.
- Have a frightening, threatening, or disconnected relationship with an accountant.
- Do the same thing year after year expecting different results.
- Unexpectedly owe taxes.

Since that final traumatic tax season, I've changed and developed into a financially literate, self-supporting, confident, and savvy woman. I still pay for annual professional help with taxes, but the experience is vastly different. Since learning practical skills and maintaining systems for tracking, planning, and integrating what happens to my money throughout the year, I am now a much more functional accounting client.

My amazing CPA, Joshua Cooper, taught me one of the most helpful lessons I ever learned as a new small-business owner: what is deductible and what isn't. He wrote the following list of general business deductions with explanations for everyday people.

Business Deductions

Advertising—Business cards, websites, social media campaigns, TV, radio, billboards, and so forth

Car Expenses—Total personal miles driven versus business miles, actual amounts paid for gas, oil changes, repairs, insurance, lease payments, and registrations

Commission/Fees Paid to Others—Contract labor

Health Insurance

Insurance—Other than health (e.g., various types of liability, natural disaster and hazard, renter's or owner's, worker's compensation, disability, property, errors and omissions, data breach, business income, and many more)

Medical and Dental Expenses—Other than health insurance

Legal, Professional, and Accounting Services—Including the amount you paid an accountant to do your taxes

Office Expenses—Items you need and use in your office (e.g., furniture, staples, paper)

Equipment—Big-ticket business items like computers, printers, phones, and the like

Studio Rental—This is not your home office. This is a space you rent for your business outside of your home, including galleries and offices.

Supplies—Specific items that you need for your business (e.g., massage lotions)

Taxes and Licenses—Other than income taxes (e.g., license renewal fees)

Travel—Hotels, planes, transportation for work, and conference fees excluding meals

Meals—All meals that are business-related, including travel meals, meals with clients, and meals by yourself in between jobs

Postage/Shipping

Telephone

Internet

Continuing Education—Classes, courses, online exams, receiving massages if you are a massage therapist, and the like

Uniform—Clothing purchased specifically for business usually needs to be protective wear, costumes, or have logos on it.

Research and Development—The cost of doing research (e.g., if you are a movie editor, going to movies is considered research)

Home Office Expenses—A percentage of your total rent and total utilities can be deducted. Provide the square footage of your office and of your total home. List your monthly rent and utilities as separate items. If you own your home, just list the square footage.

You can download the Business Deductions—Easy and Official at sfmoneycoach.com/downloads.

And then, finally, eight years into marriage with my eventual husband, I tried something I had never done before during tax season: *I delegated.* My husband completed the tax questionnaire and uploaded all of our tax-related paperwork. All I had to do was download a report of my business finances, which was fortunately a cinch, just a few clicks away. Miracle!

Holistic Approach to Debt + Savings

I know firsthand how depressing tax and consumer debt can be. A scarcity mentality can negatively affect your self-esteem, relationships, and ability to earn money. If you find yourself stuck in the debt cycle, it's more important than ever to be kind and loving with yourself and practice consistent self-care. Start with something small and jot down a list called "Ten Ways I Enjoy Taking Care of Myself" (for little or no money).

Loving yourself in these ways helps to release the tension that inevitably comes with carrying debt. If you're ready to draw the line in the sand and stop dragging around the ball and chain of past mistakes, then this section is for you. It takes discipline to pay down debt while building up savings to prevent future debt, but the sense of integrity and peace of mind you'll experience makes it worth it. Here are the strategies to save your way out of debt from the book *Financial Recovery: Developing a Healthy Relationship with Money.* Copyright © 2011 by Karen

McCall. Reprinted with permission from New World Library, Novato, CA. www.NewWorldLibrary.com.

Stop Debting

The first step toward getting out of debt is to stop digging the hole. You must stabilize the situation before you can make shifts in your mentality and changes in your behavior. Take all of your credit cards out of your wallet and then untie the cards from all of your online, phone and app-based accounts. Make sure you're paying your bills with your checking account. It is quite a project, but necessary if you're truly ready to break the cycle. Are you ready to make the event even more memorable? You can freeze your cards in a bowl of water or ceremoniously cut them up. I have a client who mailed her dad's credit card back home to him with a letter saying, "*Thank you for paying for my monthly car payments, gas, tolls, insurance and repairs for the last eight years. I'm taking on all the payments from now on!*"

Periodic Savings Account

The best antidote to credit card debt is a periodic savings account. Periodic expenses are anticipated non-monthly expenses like travel, gifts, taxes, vet bills, and car repairs. These expenses can end up on a credit card if you're not financially prepared. The periodic savings account should be a regular cash savings account with a revolving door. When a periodic expense comes up, simply transfer the money you proactively set aside back into your checking account and pay with your debit card. Sometimes, you will even deplete your periodic savings, and that's okay; it's money that is meant to be spent. By making transfers to your periodic savings account a consistent part of your monthly budget, you can build up reserves again. To calculate the goal for this savings account, map out your periodic expenses over a calendar year and divide the grand total by twelve. Periodic savings accounts are a game-changing personal finance strategy. Here's a list of the most common periodic expenses to get you started:

- Annual Charges: credit cards dues, fees, memberships, subscriptions, renewals, clubs, professional groups, stores, software
- Cars: repairs, maintenance, registration
- Clothes: seasonal shopping
- Gifts: holidays, birthdays, tips, bonuses
- Homeowners: maintenance, repairs, appliances, remodeling, improvements
- Insurance: car, homeowner's, renter's, personal property, pet, flood, earthquake, fire, etc.
- Kids: tuition, camps, birthdays
- Out-of-Pocket Medical Expenses
- Professional Services: accountant, attorney, financial planner
- Special Occasions: wedding, anniversaries, reunions, etc.
- Taxes: property, business, federal (IRS) and state
- Travel
- Vet

Manage Your Debt

Well done for taking control of the situation! The next step is living free from debt, mentally and emotionally, even if you are not technically debt-free. Now you can take an honest snapshot of your debt. Write down every balance, APR (annual percentage rate or interest rate), credit limit, minimum payment amount, and due date. To stabilize your credit score, the immediate priority is to lower every balance to a level that is at least 33 percent less than the available credit limit. Let's say your credit card limit is $10,000; you would aim for a maximum balance of $6,700, which is two-thirds of $10,000. You might plan to pay only minimums on all of your credit card accounts while you build up periodic savings and get a handle on your monthly cash flow. Others may try different strategies like a balance transfer to an interest-free credit card. I would recommend this only if it's realistic to pay it off in full before the, likely very high, interest rate hits. Some of my clients have tried a vetted debt consolidation program, a personal loan from a trusted friend or family member, the snowball method (useful for momentum), or the avalanche method (saves on interest). When creating a strategic debt repayment plan, you might need a second opinion about which approach is best for your situation from a coach, financial advisor, or accountant.

You can find links to Debt Management Tools at /resources.

Safety Net Savings Account

The next priority for cash savings is a safety net. The goal for this account is six months of living expenses. This is an emergency fund and intended for use only in case of an interruption of income. A safety net is an income backup account and provides stability and money to live on in case you're laid off, injured, go back to school, take maternity or paternity leave, need a sabbatical, a pandemic or natural disaster hits, you're set back on disability, or when you have a lower- or zero-earning month. To calculate the goal, take your average monthly burn rate, or payroll total, and multiply it by six. For example, if your typical monthly spend is $5,000, then $5,000 × 6 months = $30,000. Your safety net goal would be $30,000. Once you achieve your goal, enjoy accumulating interest in the account, which as of 2025 should be 4 to 5 percent per year.

Eliminate Debt

It's time to celebrate! You're truly free from debt financially, and now it's important to focus on integrating your emotions, spiritual perspective, and psychology about this new reality. Once all of your consumer debts are cleared, it can take some time for your heart to catch up. The key to preventing a backslide into debt is remaining connected to your money. Anyone can create a healthy and sustainable relationship with money through personal money practices, routines, rigorous honesty, willingness, and accountability.

Investments + Long-Term Savings Accounts

Let's discuss long-term savings, called investments, such as real estate, stocks, bonds, mutual funds, CDs, treasuries, retirement accounts, and more. Investments are designed to take care of your future, older self. Ideally, you would have multiple savings accounts to cover periodics, a safety net, taxes, and the long-term—so we're talking three or four separate intentional savings accounts. Remember the 1989 movie *Field of Dreams*? Build it and it will come! Something very powerful happens the moment you take action and open savings accounts, even if your initial deposits or monthly transfers are minimal. In my personal experience and having coached thousands of people in this holistic approach to debt management and savings, lasting emotional and financial security comes from building and sustaining all three levels of savings: periodics, a safety net, and investments. And remember, saving is the fastest way out of debt!

Personal Finance Routines

Now that we've covered the foundation of how personal finances work and flow, let's talk about money management, continuity, and the best practices. Financial wellness is a long game, and our relationship with money is something we all have to face and embrace, virtually every day, for the rest of our lives. Next, I want you to diagram your accounts so you can visualize how money comes in and out. Where is income deposited? Where does the majority of your spending occur? How are credit cards paid? Do you make regular transfers to savings? Do you have a separate business account? Draw it here:

Fascinating, isn't it? This picture is your garden of money and it requires water, weeding, planting and pruning to thrive. One of the primary benefits of consistently connecting with your money is finding things that need tending. Keep a running list of financial housekeeping tasks in an action plan. Here are the tried-and-true, essential routines for long-term financial wellness.

Personal Finance Routines

Weekly

- Categorize all transactions in your personal finance software—cash spending, debits, checks, automatic payments, ATM withdrawals, deposits, transfers, and all credit card charges and payments.

Mid-month

- Adjust your spending plan (budget) according to reality and make changes, if needed.
- Review your action plan.

End-of-Month

- Pay your credit cards down to zero, not just the statement balance.
- Reflect and reconcile.
- Prepare next month's spending plan before the 1st.
- Confirm that your account balances match the bank on the 1st.

Quarterly

- Update your periodic expenses calendar.
- Track your net worth.
- Adjust your annual spending plan.

Annually

- At the end of the year, reflect on your relationship with money. What went well? What was challenging? What do you want to address and accomplish next year?
- Complete your annual spending plan by February 1st.
- Create a timeline for tax season by February 1st.

You can download the Personal Finance Routines at sfmoneycoach.com/downloads.

Working with Resistance

Is this all too much? Are you pushing down feelings of rebellion, anger, stress, or sadness? At this juncture, you may be thinking, *Yeah right, as if I'll do any of this* or, *I just can't.* Your feelings are valid and if resistance crops up, offer yourself some compassion by saying to the Universe, *Help me hold my thoughts and emotions with loving-kindness.* And, remember that setbacks are normal and part of the change process.

I had one client who was born in extreme poverty, in a small house with a dirt floor and an unreliable roof. Her mother was a teenage mom at only thirteen years old. She had two dresses and one pair of shoes with holes in them. They bounced from shelter to shelter and even slept in hairsalons sometimes when her mom was able to keep a cleaning job. Miraculously, my client managed to get an education. She made her way through high school, college, and even graduate school on scholarships. She worked hard and made a ton of money in high-end real estate.

In our first session, she told me she felt "allergic to money." She had a deep pattern of feast-or-famine and couldn't hold onto her money for long enough between fluctuating paychecks. She said building savings to carry over from one job to another was out of the question. In her circle of friends in Chicago, she was a highflier. She would receive comission checks of tens of thousands of dollars at once and take her closest girlfriends out for five-star dinners and treat everyone. We covered practical topics like creating a budget, the ABCs and 123s of personal finance, communicating with friends, and strategically paying off back taxes. We also talked about what reparenting her inner child would look like. She admitted she needed to abstain from pot which, for her, always led to alcohol use followed by too much drinking and then it was "off to the races and we'd stay out all night on my dime!" She was the kindest, most warm-hearted person, and I coached her through five or so paycheck cycles and then she invariably ran up the balance on her overdraft credit card account. Even though I did my best to provide her with tools, education, empowerment, and support, I believe that her own shame, and possible addictions, got in the way of change; resistance won out, and she no-showed for appointments twice in a row before she stopped contacting me.

Here's another client story about resistance. Simone was a former professional ice-skater and three years away from inheriting a life-changing trust. She had a good job as an associate lawyer and lived in Denver, a relatively affordable city. However, she spent more than she earned every month. During the first session, I suggested that she separate her personal finances from her work expenses. Every month, she was required to charge thousands of dollars of reimbursable business expenses on a personal card. She resisted designating one card for business use only, but I could see how combining personal and work expenses on one credit card was exacerbating her money fog and magical thinking. And she was really attached to the miles. Every time we attempted to talk through her credit card balances and the true cost of her life, she had to do complex mental gymnastics to sort through her accounts. Instead of taking what I would describe as *low-hanging fruit*, she tried to reduce her overall spending by selling sports equipment, taking on a side hustle instructing children in figure skating, researching and negotiating for lower insurance premiums, and cohabitating with her boyfriend.

However, the math still didn't work. She incurred expensive but avoidable interest charges month after month. She longed for the days of being a sponsored skater and hanging out at the rink all day, and frequently reminisced that she had "no problems" during those years. Her affluent parents had bailed her out of credit card debt multiple times in the past, but this last time, they made it an interest-free loan and Simone owed them $1,000 per month in repayment. The final reimbursement would be paid off in full the month before her inheritance. Throughout our work together, she never broke the debt cycle. In fact, because her expenses were so muddled, I never really knew exactly how much she owed and I am not sure she ever knew either. Though clearly struggling emotionally and financially, she dug her heels in, resisted my suggestions, and simply refused to make small changes to help herself. One day, I lovingly but directly asked her what the payoff was for commingling her personal and work expenses year after year. Silence ensued.... We wrapped up the session and I never heard from her again. I've thought about her many times and. only wish I had more time to offer different interventions, more skillfully help her process what she was hiding or hiding from, and to refer her to other professionals. If I had the chance to work with either of these women again, I might ask the following questions that are effective for loosening the grip of resistance:

On a scale from one to ten, where one is that you're not managing your money at all (avoidant) and ten means you're managing your money very well (vigilant), how would you rate the job you're doing managing your money today?

On a scale from one to ten, with one representing that you are not willing to change anything and ten meaning you are willing to do whatever it takes to sort things out, where do you see yourself right now?

What do you want to learn, improve or expand in your financial life?

____

____

____

____

____

What is one thing you need to change or let go of?

____

____

How has the pain around this changed you as a person?

What are the best possible results if you do make the changes?

What do you fear in making these changes?

How would you like things to turn out ten years from now?

____

____

____

____

____

What might happen in the next five to ten years if you don't make these changes?

____

____

____

____

____

No matter how hard I tried, some of my clients clung onto their self-destructive behaviors and negative mindsets for dear life—as if they were carrying around a stinky old teddy bear with a missing eye, stuffing coming out, and ripped clothes. It takes courage to put the bear down and break through. Facing your fears can be scary. You may need support in opening up—whether that comes from your best financial friend (BFF), nature, guided meditations, music, bodywork, or another resource. There are facets of human psychology beyond my scope as a money coach, and I often give referrals to licensed therapists when a person's health care needs demand outside professional care. Whoever you choose to lean on should be trustworthy, nonjudgmental, and compassionate. And your resistance have some important messages, memories, or lessons for you. Try to mine the gold!

Now, back to setting yourself up for success. Once your system is customized and up and running, you're golden. You've pushed the boulder up the hill. As you know, the foundational routine to maintain financial wellness is categorizing all of your transactions one or two times per week, a.k.a. reviewing your spending. If you cannot keep this up consistently, you might need to hire a bookkeeper. I hired one, myself, for a two-year period—even after I had been teaching people how to keep their own books for over a decade. For me, the realities of working, parenting two children under five, breastfeeding the baby, required weekly volunteering at their co-op preschool, managing my physical health with an autoimmune disorder, a flailing competitive tennis career, and commuting across the country to see my own aging parents, there was simply no way I could *do it all* without losing my mind. A bookkeeper became as essential for me as a housekeeper, and I am so grateful to the entire Jenny Abbott Company team for their loving support during that time. And even if you're just plain busy or simply don't want to do it, those are also valid reasons to outsource tracking and bookkeeping as soon as possible.

If you dare to take these steps and consistently engage with your spending plan, you may be in the minority of people you know. It's okay to be different. And it can be fun and even pleasurable to be an outlier in this realm. Go to any lengths to take care of yourself and be a good steward of your money. Remember, suffering is optional!

Chapter Three

Analyzing

The next level of financial wellness is learning to analyze your decisions, patterns, and behaviors. Analysis, translated as *dhamma vicaya*,, involves understanding the difference between what you thought would happen and what did happen. And, when overspending occurs, work to understand the *reason* for overspending. In this chapter, I'll share a personal story of self-acceptance and learning to be "At Home Within." Remember, the goal here is progress, not perfection.

Five Reasons We Overspend

Even for families with two full-time working parents, after the mortgage, childcare, student loans, and monthly credit card bills, it can sometimes feel impossible to fund a vacation, do a modest remodel, or keep up with the kids' wardrobe needs—not to mention our own! The pressure is even more intense if you're single or if one parent stays at home. Part of my job as a financial coach is to help families identify and stop leaks in spending and curb overspending. I was surprised to discover the most common reasons we overspend:

Periodics
Income
Planning
Emotions
and
Drumroll please…
Credit Cards

1. Periodics—As we discussed, a periodic expense is an *anticipated* non-monthly expense. Examples are taxes, gifts, insurance, car repairs, household maintenance, vet bills, travel, and more. People tend to get flustered when one of these "have-to" expenses *suddenly* pops up. Being financially savvy requires planning ahead, taking preventive measures, and preparing for surprises.

   What you can do: Create and maintain a calendar of scheduled and potential periodic expenses over the course of a calendar year. Divide the grand total by twelve to calculate a monthly savings goal. Set aside money into a designated periodic expenses savings account every month and use the funds when a periodic expense occurs.
2. Income—Payday is not a good day to go shopping. While many people feel a certain freedom when a paycheck posts or direct deposit hits their account, that money is largely spoken for. Without a realistic budget, you will never really know how much you can spend. *Pay yourself first* means prioritizing your savings goals

right away. Automate your savings! In doing so, you'll reduce friction and harness the status quo bias, which leads us to keep things the way they are.

What you can do: Pause when you get paid. Create a plan for how you want to allocate each paycheck—a.k.a., a budget. If you're lucky enough to receive extra or sudden money like a bonus, tax refund, inheritance, stock option sale, commission, gift, and other fluctuating income, consider the Rule of Thirds: 33 percent goes to the past, 33 percent for the present, and put 33 percent away for the future. Create a periodic income calendar so you can plan around fluctuations and know, as much as possible, what to expect when.

3. Planning—Rushing and underestimating are common causes of overspending. Don't wait until you're on your way to a party to buy a host gift—plan ahead. This discipline can save you hundreds if not thousands of dollars a year. Do your best to be an informed consumer and avoid falling into the quicksand of overspending like a client of mine did. "I thought new tires would cost $400, but the total bill was $686 with alignment, recycling fees, taxes, and same-day service."

   What you can do: Research upcoming expenses. Call ahead. Take a few minutes every month to be proactive. Scan your calendar while creating your spending plan. Have at least two money dates with your honey or best financial friend (BFF) every month. Know how much money you need in your accounts each week as well as at the end of the month.

4. Emotional—Retail therapy, anyone? Human beings are highly motivated by pleasure and extremely averse to

> pain. People will do virtually anything to fill the God-sized hole in their heart and seek release—*moksha*—from tension in a variety of ways, including spending on food, drinks, media, clothes, technology, travel, entertainment, hobbies, other people, and more. Your emotional state will impact on the final bill. There may be an initial high from the purchases; unfortunately, emotional spending can leave you feeling guilt-ridden or worse.

One day, my mother-in-law burst through our shared front door from Costco, beaming and flushed, with a long receipt in her hand, yelling, "Six-hundred and two dollars! Can you believe it?!" She was *buzzed* from the shopping excursion, having, for instance, purchased fifteen pounds of treats for our fourteen-pound dog. She clearly found the price point and the "good deal" intoxicating. This is the same person who became very angry when I tossed a single spoonful of week-old food from the fridge. I do have compassion for her though. Sylvia grew up in Johannesburg, South Africa, during apartheid. Her parents did not have much money to raise three girls. They had a tin roof, handsewn clothes, and a homemade electricity network with wires dangling from the ceiling. She worked very, very hard to graduate from college and get to America, where she earned a PhD.

At the age of thirty-five, an immigrant single mother of two boys, ages five and ten, she was accepted into medical school. Sylvia then earned her MD and had a long career as a general practitioner at Kaiser. She retired on my first child's due date and has been very successful studying about and managing her own investments ever since. Yet, her financial behavior baffles me on a daily basis. Switching back and forth between extreme frugality and gross overspending may be due to jumping social classes. Since we're all just cavepeople at heart, whose brains haven't had an upgrade in hundreds of thousands of years, I am sure she feels deep emotions around money, even today when she is "set" for life. I imagine she may be traumatized by the experience of leaving her home country, her subsequent divorce, and acclimating to a new stage of wealth can be emotionally wrought for folks. At the same time, Sylvia is incredibly, boundlessly generous with her own family. I do my very best to step back and just witness her without judgment and without trying to change anything. I try to remember and appreciate her rags-to-riches story and have respect and admiration for everything she's manifested and endured in her life.

> What you can do: Understand that people can be driven to spend compulsively due to stress, low self-esteem, anxiety, and even depression. Tune in to your feelings more often, especially around spending decisions. Are you calm, relaxed, and in a state of equanimity? Or are you dysregulated, triggered, fearful, or Hungry, Angry, Lonely, Tired (HALT)? Start by identifying patterns in your binge spending. It may be an opportunity to uncover an unmet need.

I have a client who is a chronic overspender. Her weaknesses are clothes, bags, shoes, and jewelry. She has expensive taste and virtually can't say no to Bergdorf Goodman salespeople who know her by name at the 5th Avenue location in New York. I gave her a tool she could always carry with her: a mini paper spending journal. Over time, she developed self-awareness through daily spiritual practices and discovered she had an ability to slow down and record the details of her compulsive shopping experiences. She would document her feelings before, during, and after and the tool helped her connect to her underlying thoughts and beliefs. Through this process, she realized she was feeling lonely and bored on the way home from work and frequently stopped in at Bergdorf's to pass time and have social interaction. The unmet need was in her social life and relationships. She compensated for that void by overspending on her wardrobe.

Anyone who has been in debt knows how quickly things can get out of control. Be mindful of slippery slopes, hot-spot areas of spending, and your triggers. In the yoga community, we talk about *samskaras*, or habits. Self-destructive habits must be restructured and replaced with something healthy. And it turns out there's only one thing that can fill the God-sized hole in your heart, and that's your personal version of a Higher Power.

Financial Psychology Research

With compulsive buying disorder, there is an underlying belief that [acquiring] objects will create happiness and act as a vehicle for improving one's moods. Although moods can improve during the shopping experience and briefly exist after acquiring a product, the feeling is often short-lived and may be followed by negative feelings of guilt, depression, and lower self-esteem.

You can cleanse yourself of guilt by selling unused, unwanted, or shameful items. Keep a list of healthy stress relievers. Develop daily practices that provide you with a sense of grounding and clear thinking, such as meditation, intentions (prayers), inspirational reading, or mindful breathing. I recently discovered my health insurance, and my local library, lend free subscriptions to the Calm app with no expiration date. While it may be tempting to throw your budget out the window after a bad retail therapy day, remember your goals and that you're the author of your own financial success story. Lastly, experiment with recording the circumstances and your emotions in a spending journal. To overcome the compulsion to spend, you may need the help of a doctor, therapist, or other professional.

Resources and Support for Compulsive Spending can be found at sfmoneycoach.com/resources.

5. Credit Cards—One study by Prelec and Simester of MIT found that people overspend as much as 100 percent of the time on credit cards. PWe're all at risk for overspending on daily purchases simply by using a credit card over a debit card or cash. In addition to potential interest charges on the balance, which can be as high as 29.99 percent each month, if you're not paying attention, anyone could inadvertently overspend. As if this wasn't alarming enough, heavy credit card use can exacerbate: debt, financial vagueness, magical thinking, compulsive spending, and underearning too.

   What you can do: Try one month, or better yet, ninety days, without using credit cards. Journal about the impact on your cash flow and money consciousness. If that bridge is just too long, at the very least, consolidate all new charges to one active card. Be intentional and practice healthy credit card use by paying off your actual balances, down to zero, every month rather than just paying the statement balance. Even then, there will still be a disconnect between acquiring, booking, or purchasing something and the reality of paying for it.

> Last, if you are harboring a secret credit card, it's time to come clean to the people you love and who love you. Don't allow truth management to keep you separate; you'd be succumbing to power and control dynamics rather than offering and exercising trust.

Because you're human, overspending is inevitable sometimes. Responsibility means "able to respond" and financially savvy people pause to reflect on the reason. Prosperity doesn't just happen; it takes time, discipline, and recognition that you have more choice and power in your financial life than you realized. Remember HOW this works: Honesty, Open-Mindedness, and Willingness are the keys to success.

Shop in Your Own Closet

Do you love shopping a little too much? Does spending money trigger feelings of urgency, regret, guilt, or even intoxication? It's time to slow down. If you are obsessed with clothes, try shopping in your own closet. A financial therapist ordered me to perform this powerful exercise "before you spend any more money on clothes". I was surprised by the medicinal effects. Shopping in my own closet proved to be a strong antidote to both impulsive and compulsive shopping. The assignment was to take a complete inventory of my entire wardrobe, which required emptying every single drawer and pulling all the clothes, jackets, and accessories out of my closet. It was suggested to keep a notepad handy to record totals, and keep a running list of specific wardrobe needs that come up.

Sort the contents of your wardrobe into five piles:

Keep
Donate
Throw Away
Sell
Repair

1. Keep items only if you can easily say, "I love it, I wear it, and it fits." Beware of any wishful thinking like, "Maybe someday…" Just say no!
2. Donate anything you haven't worn in the last year. Has it been over a year? It definitely has to go. The only exceptions would be particularly sentimental items and special occasion clothes. Put them in a garment bag in the back of your closet. Schedule a calendar reminder to review this decision in a year.
3. Throw away pieces that don't fit, you never wear, are permanently stained, or are otherwise inappropriate for someone else to wear. Toss them!
4. Try selling or consigning anything of value: jackets, jewelry, your Jimmy Choo heels collection (true story from a client), and other once-loved items that don't resonate with a clear *yes*. You can try TheRealReal, ThredUp, Poshmark, and eBay, for starters.
5. Repair, mend, and fix items you otherwise won't wear. Sort items that need hemming, ironing, new buttons, or other alterations. Once you properly maintain and sort your existing wardrobe, it will feel wonderfully new again.

The first time I did this, the sheer number of pants, shoes, and bags was overwhelming, and I literally found items hidden in the clutter that I loved but had forgotten about. It was helpful to invite a friend over for vetting and emotional support. Vacuum the dust balls and wipe down the shelves. You may need to get some new thin hangers, bins, boxes, or boot inserts. Commit to finishing the project even if you need to take a break, run an errand for supplies, or return to it tomorrow. Put each item back in a way that makes sense. Some people love sorting their clothes by type, season, color, and sleeve length. Now, tackle your drawers, accessories, shoes, and coats as well. Once you reorganize and spruce everything up, you'll have a complete list of everything you truly need *and* feel awesome and inspired every time you go to get dressed. Prioritize your honest shopping needs, and choose one affordable item to start with this month. You deserve it!

Twelve Money Disorders

My colleague and mentor, Dr. Brad Klontz, PsyD, CFP®, categorizes twelve money disorders into three groupings: Money Avoidance, Money Worship, and Relational Money Disorders. Let's explore these not as a diagnostic exercise, but a way in which to shed light on how common disordered behavior is and to offer a gentle warning that the more attached you are to these beliefs, the more serious the potential consequences.

People who fall into the trappings of Money Avoidance sometimes believe they are undeserving of money and attempt to fashion a lifestyle of "noble poverty." Because of their negative associations with money and wealth, Money Avoiders may sabotage their financial success, compulsively spend, or give money away in an unconscious effort to have as little as possible. You might have a Money Avoidance script if you ignore bank statements, have difficulty sticking to a budget, or feel overwhelming angst about others' beliefs or practices with money. Here are the most common thought patterns correlated to Money Avoidance:

- Financial denial—*It's best to not think about money.*
- Financial rejection—*Money is the root of all evil. People who care about money are corrupt, greedy, and bad.*
- Excessive risk aversion—*I will never trust anyone else with my money.*
- Underspending—*It's extravagant to spend money on myself.*

On the other end of the spectrum, Money Worshippers are convinced that more money and more possessions will make them happy and solve their problems. At the same time, they believe they will never have enough. These individuals are likely to have lower income, lower net worth, and carry credit card debt. Money Worshippers may fall into patterns of:

- Compulsive hoarding—*There will never be enough.*
- Workaholism—*I have to work hard to make sure there's enough money. I have to be busy all the time to feel like I'm enough.*
- Unreasonable risk-taking or pathological gambling—*If I just keep trying, my day will come.*
- Overspending or compulsive buying—*I need this now. I need to purchase multiples of a good find.*

Relational Money Disorders are tangled up with dynamics, secrets, and dishonesty. Money is a deep source of shame for many people; that's why it remains such a taboo topic. Money is so powerful, it can easily become an instrument of control or even abuse. Individuals suffering from Relational Money Disorders wreak havoc on their own emotional and financial lives as well as those of their loved ones. Parents, in particular, face the balancing act of sharing but not burdening their children with too many details or lengthy descriptions of family difficulties. People with Relational Money Disorders may give money to others even when they can't afford it, which can look like:

- Financial infidelity—*It's okay to keep secrets from my partner about money.*
- Financial incest—*Spending money on someone is how I show love.*
- Financial enabling—*If I hold others financially responsible, they will reject me.*
- Financial dependence—*There will always be someone I can turn to for money.*

Do any of these money disorders, behaviors, or lines of thinking resonate or sound all too familiar? I can think of at least twenty people in my immediate circle who suffer from financial disorders. One of my clients is single, has never had children, and is ultrawealthy by inheritance. Yet, she lives in a tiny apartment, denying herself long-overdue upgrades and fixes. She spends hours every week poring over her spending, balancing her checkbook to every last penny of the small amount she's allotted herself to live on. I have another client who feels stuck in a highly stressful job he hates, works around the clock, has poor health, and negatively affected family relationships. Yet, he refuses to complete the necessary steps to get help, explore change, or receive financial advice from any professionals. I have two unrelated women clients who are actively hiding credit card debt from their husbands by managing secret charge accounts out of their businesses. Coincidentally, they are both licensed therapists. Is there anything inherently wrong with any of these people? Absolutely not. And I have zero judgment of their choices and situations, just compassion and hope.

Here are seven ways to improve your financial health today:

1. Get professional guidance from a local or online therapist, behaviorist, coach, counselor, accountant, financial planner, attorney, or social worker.
2. Join a money-related twelve-step program. This is a zero cost optionfor codependents, debtors, gamblers, underearners, spenders, bettors, workaholics, and more. Links can be found at sfmoneycoach.com/resources.
3. Lean on your BFF (best financial friend) and tell the truth about your behavior, needs, and financial goals.
4. Apply the Three As: Awareness, Acceptance, Action. First, admit you are powerless over ________ = *Awareness*. Believe that there is a solution and you can be restored to sanity = *Acceptance*. Make a decision to change your behavior = *Action*.
5. Write out a clear communication plan for cleaning up past mistakes
6. Address wishy-washy personal or business loans including a start date, schedule, amounts, and delivery method.
7. Pray and meditate.

Remember, isolation is not a solution, and no situation is truly hopeless. No matter what the circumstances, it is possible to feel happy and confident in your relationship with money, one day at a time.

Financial Psychology

This section explores my own personal financial psychology and how the lessons I've learned can be applied to life. What follows is a discussion of: financial flashpoints, my own money scripts, more on my family history, and practical solutions and tools.

Financial Flashpoints

Exploring financial flashpoints can provide you with important clues as to why you do what you do with money. A flashpoint is a significant event from the past that shapes your attitude and behavior. These experiences are so emotionally powerful, the imprints usually last through adulthood. Ask yourself:

Can you draw a symbol of your earliest money memory?

What is your most joyful money memory?

What is your most painful memory with money?

As you've already heard, before I made the decision to become educated and empowered about money, I made a ton of mistakes. In surveying my life, I recalled my earliest money memory was helping my dad roll change. He had all the differently sized empty brown-paper coin rolls. I sorted the change, counted the coins, folded the cylindrical envelopes around the loot, and promptly gave my dad's money back to him. My most joyful money memory was receiving my first real paycheck at age thirteen. After years of being a mother's helper and babysitter for cash, when my sister left for college, I took over her job serving breakfast to parishioners at our family's church. The first time I got a printed check in the mail, written out to my name, I was ecstatic!

My most painful money memory was the first time I realized my dad did not approve of the shopping sprees my mom took me on. I remember where I was standing in the front hall, caught with bags on the stairs, and I felt disappointed and ashamed. Every time I wore the items, I was riddled with guilt over my dad's overt unhappiness. I was conflicted since I had such a huge desire and need for the clothes.

I will never know if these potent financial flashpoints triggered some, or all, of my dysfunctional behavior around money, but here are some of the ways in which I think I was affected.

Underearning Career Path—After college, my first full-time job was at Town School for Boys in Pacific Heights, as an intern teacher, earning an annual gross salary of $18,000. Now, living in San Francisco, I took on second, third, and fourth jobs tutoring, coaching, babysitting, and leading outdoor adventure trips in the summer to supplement my income.

I received a $1,000 gift from my family each year, and I acknowledge how fortunate I am that my family had those resources. However, the mixed messages and emotional consequences of interacting with my parents about money grew increasingly difficult. My mom paid for plane tickets home to Michigan without hesitation; however, every single time, my dad scolded me, demanding to be included in making the decisions. While my mom experienced joy with money and celebrated life by spending, my dad was very frugal, constantly grumpy about money, and, as the sole earner, he worked...*a lot.*

Moving Addiction—I graduated from college in 1997 and moved eighteen times in the subsequent fifteen years. I was constantly on the go, searching for locations where the grass was greener. I was always seeking to improve my life, my relationships, my living situation, and myself. Moving is expensive, and I repeatedly tapped into my meager teacher's retirement account to fund the project—not a healthy plan or something I'd recommend to anyone. There was the first and last month's rent, the security deposit, paying movers since, at some point, I just couldn't ask my friends for help again. And, there were always last-minute add-ons like start-up costs for utilities and buying furniture that fit the new place.

Compulsive Shopping—I had (have) a little spending streak, particularly when busy, which was all the time. My schedule didn't allow adequate time for finding bargains or browsing for beautiful items that not only fit well but were functional. I'd call myself a *seasonal shopper* and would spend $1,000 to $2,000 on clothes for myself at once, just like my mom would. On a teacher's salary, this was unrealistic and out of proportion triggering credit card use and a negative self-image. Often, my new clothes required pricey alterations as well to fit my pear-shaped body.

I had no clue how to make decisions based in reality. But I do know, I still don't enjoy shopping to this day.

Overspending—It took me several years to forgive myself for hiring an out-of-state accountant to start an S corp. I was between teaching jobs, attempting to start a tutoring business, and working for myself for the first time. It was terrible advice, since I wasn't anywhere close to netting over $100,000—the suggested minimum to make an S corp worthwhile in California. I wasted thousands of dollars on the S corp setup and closure fees. I was naive and immature and felt completely powerless at the mercy of a corrupt authority figure.

Pyramid Scheme—I invested $5,000 cash, again from my retirement account, in a pyramid scheme couched as a "feminine economy" a.k.a., *The Garden*. The commitment carried a promise of cashing out with an eightfold payback of $40,000, and I personally knew several women who had gone all the way through the center and received the payout. I did it for the possibility that I, too, would cash out. I jumped in without thinking, but, like many pyramid schemes, success is based on recruitment. I tried to bring people in and hung on for dear life for two years. Ultimately, I pulled out of the circle and lost every dollar. Admittedly, it wasn't a complete disaster, since one result was hyperbonding with a new group of friends into *manifestation* like me. Manifestation, one of my favorite topics, is the art of making something theoretical, like a vision, desire, or a job real.

Money Scripts and Family History

Evaluating my financial psychology was an emotional turning point. After completing the Klontz Money Script Inventory, myself, I was shocked to learn my highest scores were in Money Worship *and* Money Status. When I've done money personality tests in the past, I usually come up with the "bookkeeper" type and was sure I'd prove to be Money Vigilant! I was a student of Dr. Brad Klontz at the time, and he explained that money scripts are learned in childhood, typically unconsciously, passed down from generation to generation, and often just partial truths. Money scripts are not only a good way to externalize some of your core beliefs, but understanding them can impact financial outcomes like increasing your income, net worth, and improving financial health. You had me at *increase*, Brad!

On a scale of one to six, my Money Worship score was a four, suggesting that I exhibited many of the characteristics of this money script. Still to this day, I tend to spend a bit compulsively since I don't make time to enjoy myself. I squeeze it in whenever possible and get it over with. I imagine I don't love shopping because of the mixed messages from my parents. My mom overdoing it every time on the one hand and my dad cringing and punishing us by being mean, withdrawing, and withholding love.

I have to give myself credit for being good at purging and throwing things away. I am not a hoarder. I do make annual donations, as much as I can scrape together, to various institutions. I was partially financially dependent on my husband, by only working part-time, since I cared for our kids when they got home from school. By this time, I did not have credit card debt anymore, something that many money worshippers do have.

My score on the Money Status scale was 1.57, suggesting that I *do not* hold strong money status beliefs. In retrospect, I can see that my parents were humble. Even though we had an amazingly privileged life with private school, tennis camps, country club memberships, and vacations in Florida every year, we also lived simply by playing outside in the backyard, raking our own leaves, and going for family walks. My parents would point out our neighbors, like the actual Ford family heirs, who apparently had much more money than us. This wasn't a good or bad thing; it was just how it was. We lived in an affluent suburb but were still in the middle class.

My Money Vigilance score was three, indicating that I *do not* strongly endorse Money Vigilance characteristics. I had hoped this would be my strongest money script. I was a financial coach, after all! Money Vigilant people are supposedly very alert, aware, and concerned about their financial welfare. And, after getting help with money, I went for years without spending on credit. I have seen signs of deprivation in my own life where, for some reason, I virtually cannot spend money on something I need. I used to be into cycling and had clip-in bike shoes that were disintegrating so much that I would return from rides with tiny pieces of green plastic from the shoes covering my calves. I did eventually replace them but after a few years of living like this. My inclination to do without and make do is a mysterious block I still grapple with.

My score on the Money Avoidance scale was 1.5, suggesting that I *did not* exhibit significant Money Avoidance beliefs. Phew! And that would make sense since I had been committed to my own financial wellness journey for ten years at that point.

By peeling back the layers of my own financial psychology, I uncovered a strong belief that *parents owe their children the truth and emotional availability.* Truth-telling was sadly not a value in my family of origin. Our family valued doing over being, and we existed within a closed system, with no feedback. There was virtually no processing, repair, or reflecting on relationships, communication nuances, or life challenges. Breakdowns kind of just happened and we all went on with the day. There was an unspoken "no-talk rule"—especially when it came to finances. I believe this led me to stay numb most of the time, to not allow my own negative feelings (or those of others), to not believe my eyes, and to not trust myself or others with money. Plus, as the third child of four and a girl, there were additional strikes against me. What I witnessed growing up was a lot of sugarcoating, triangulation, and a big focus on how we presented ourselves to the community: brush your hair, dress properly, say nice things, act appropriately, and date people from the right families. Many teenagers go through a period of conflict with their parents. I alternated between bouts of my mother's silent treatment over my rebellious behavior and compartmentalizing aspects of myself seeking approval from my dad. I remained tightly-wound, entitled, angry at the world, and deeply entrenched in a state of isolation, martyrdom, and victimhood. I tried various ways to push back and release my teenage angst: shoplifting, smoking cigarettes, making out, swearing, lying, refusing to shave, going braless, and cheating at school. Fortunately and unfortunately, there were minimal consequences, if any at all. I was selfish, self-loathing, self-centered, and even petulant well beyond the typical teenage years. I was disgruntled from age sixteen to twenty-six. It wasn't until I got help from therapists and twelve-step-based group therapy that I started to see my part, take responsibility, and begin cleaning up my side of the street.

Hands down, the number one value my parents instilled in me was that *I was loveable*. I know today that my parents did the best they could with what they had. My older brother and sister definitely broke them in for me, and the bottom line was that no matter what I did, they would always love me no matter what. I could really feel that was true growing up, and still sense and believe it today. This value is also expressed by the fact that my parents were married until my mom died. How a man and woman can fight over money for over fifty years and remain together is beyond me. My dad was the earner, and my mom was the spender. It seems like every financial decision they made was wrought with pain for both of them. Imagine living like that! Once the youngest was off to college, the four of us kids sat down with our parents and literally told them it was okay to get divorced now. They laughed it off and uttered a quintessential waspy statement "We're *fine*!"

So how does one recover from painful memories, past mistakes, mixed messages from parents, financial dependence, and deeply embedded money scripts? Through honesty, open-mindedness, and willingness to learn, make changes, and practice radical acceptance.

Celebrate the Good

Since the *aha* moment the week of my thirtieth birthday when I realized I needed financial help, I have accomplished a lot. I have successfully learned how to balance a checkbook, build and maintain savings for periodic expenses. I even opened an additional retirement account, a SEP IRA, for myself, and a Roth IRA for each of my children. I *still* categorize all of my spending in a sophisticated financial tracking software program, track my net worth, and analyze my budget versus actuals each month and annually.

I addressed my underearning issues and areas of chronic deprivation. After uncovering just how toxic, unattractive, and draining indebtedness was for me, I stopped using credit cards altogether. No longer a victim, I faced my past with money, which was something I had been actively running from for a decade. With newly cultivated tools, strength, and a sense of responsibility and awareness, I became able to participate in adult conversations about money again. Thanks to Barbara Huson, who gave me my first *receiving journal*, I learned to celebrate the good, which includes celebrating others' success and happiness without falling into compare and despair. Receiving could mean anything from opening the mail to seeing that direct deposit hit your account. An opportunity to confront a financially dependent family member or completing a financial housekeeping task like following up on an unknown charge. I cultivated a deep sense of confidence, gratitude, and connection to the Universe writing in this journal almost every day for two years. The discipline invited me to be present, notice beauty, and acknowledge what I had, what went well, and what felt good each day. There are many ways to shift from a poverty mentality to a wealthy mindset, but gratitude is probably the easiest and most readily accessible. A daily gratitude practice can change your brain structure and lead to a more fulfilling experience as a human being.

Make Amends

There had been a time when I was looking for a fix, an escape—anything but my mundane teenage 1990s life in a Christian, country-club family. And shoplifting worked. This type of risk-taking gave me a certain sense of danger and adventure, and I loved all the scheming and planning. The dopamine rush was guaranteed because I always got away with it. There were no cameras tracking your every move back then.

My biggest heist was at an outdoor shopping center in Glen Arbor, Michigan. My friends and I found a large box behind the stores near the employee parking lot. We divided and conquered and each hit three or four stores, grabbing whatever we could confiscate in our large overcoats, pockets, and hands. It was just so easy. With our naive looks, we worked slowly, consciously, and with discipline. We stole clothes, pouches, hacky sacks, lighters, and cheap jewelry. It was entertainment and it felt free.

In addition to squaring off with my history of shoplifting, I faced my entire financial history without fainting, and the grip of anxiety in my solar plexus slowly lifted. Various mentors helped me look at the psychological, emotional, and spiritual sides of money and be honest about *everything*. I was finally able to identify and resolve my problems. My teachers listened compassionately while I confessed my resistance and past mistakes like gross overspending, losing money, lying about money, vandalizing property, and actual theft. Over time, I made direct amends and repaid each and every store I had ever stolen from, which looked like making donations and mailing cash with anonymous apology letters to Laura Ashley headquarters in London, England, souvenier shops in Carmel, California and various stores "up north" and in my hometown. I believe that making amends, with the help of my Al-Anon sponsor, lifted a huge weight and allowed me to start living with purpose, grace, dignity, and respect again.

Be Here Now

The very first time I intentionally meditated, it was an assignment from my college professor, Elli Findly. The first class for my major in religion was called Buddhism 101 and, in order to pass, we were expected to attend an open meditation at the Hartford Karma Thegsum Choling Center on Elizabeth Street. I found the temple, altar, wall hangings, Buddhist images, and saffron and maroon monks' robes stunningly gorgeous and colorful, unlike the cold, Gothic, gray stone church I grew up in. Sitting in silence was, of course, difficult and a bit unnerving.I'll never forget a monk sitting on the next cushion and teaching me what is commonly practiced in seated meditation. *Dhyana mudra* is a hand gesture of enlightenment and wisdom. Place palms up in your lap, rest the right hand on top of the left, and gently touch your thumbs together to form a circle. I remember returning to campus reveling with a sense of wonder from the sacred experience.

Years later, I dipped my toes back into meditation when a boyfriend lent me a complete set of Holosync CDs (compact discs). Using noise-canceling headphones, I soaked my mind in the sounds of nature compiled with beta, alpha, theta, and delta brainwave patterns for an hour a day. Needless to say, my proclivity for meditation lasted longer than the relationship.

Later still, looking for social opportunities outside of bars, I frequented the San Francisco Zen Center on Page Street a.k.a., Beginner's Mind Temple, *Hosshin-ji*, as well as its sister property, Green Gulch Farm and Zen Center, in Marin County on weekends. On Friday nights, I enjoyed Dharma Punx, which consisted of a forty-five-minute dharma talk and a forty-five-minute silent meditation. I love these thought-provoking philosophical discussions on aspects of truth and reality.

I was practicing yoga at least three times a week at the time. I loved the practice immensely and felt more at home on the mat than most other places. On a whim, I signed up for the five-hundred-hour yoga teacher training program at my home studio, The Yoga Loft on Divisadero. We studied *asanas* (yoga postures), the history of yoga, the *yamas* and *niyamas* (social ethics and moral codes in yoga), Patanjali's *Yoga Sutras* (philosophy), *pranayama* (breathing techniques), anatomy, physiology, yoga therapy, sequencing, teaching methodology, Ayurvedic medicine principles, and we chanted in Sanskrit. A teacher there mentioned another style of meditation called *Vipassana*, a word in the ancient language of Pali, which means *seeing things as they really are*.

After completing the yearlong yoga intensive and attempting to maintain my newly healthy lifestyle, I registered for a ten-day silent Vipassana meditation retreat near the south fork of the American River. Each of the ten days began with the 4 a.m. wake-up bell, followed by ten hours of meditation interspersed with breaks and rest periods until the day ended at 9 p.m. There were no phones allowed, no technology at all, not even books, journals, or reading material of any kind. We ate like monks, having light, simple, vegetarian meals. Everything we did—from walking meditation, eating in silence, abstaining from eye contact, refraining from giving or responding to mistaken social cues, to just resting in our bunk beds for a few hours each night—allowed for a deep and significant operation on the mind. Until childbirth many years later, being completely silent and largely sitting still for ten days was the most difficult thing I had ever done.

One night, while more in a state of *savasana*, or corpse pose, than sleep, I dreamed that my friend Alicia was with my ex-boyfriend James in Los Angeles. They enjoyed a cheese tray together and talked about his laptop being stolen. I thought nothing of it except, *How random!* In the days back home following the ten-day sit, I was catching up with friends on the phone. I called Alicia in Oakland and told her about my dream. She was silent. Then, *Carrie, you're not going to believe this. While you were gone, I took a spontaneous road trip to LA. I called James out of the blue and he invited me over for a drink. We sat on his balcony and ate a beautiful cheese tray together. He told me a story about accidentally leaving his laptop in his car overnight and that it had been stolen.* I started screaming and running around, exhilarated. I had dreamed the exact details of my friend's actual life from four hundred miles away. I believe I may have experienced astral projection, a journey of the soul. Either way, this *oneness* phenomenon, non-duality, was an undeniable sign that *everything is connected.*

Many years later, while living under the same roof and daily scrutiny of my in-laws, around-the-clock nursing eight-week-old Max, managing a remodel (to build him a bedroom), attempting to return to work, and in the throes of grief from my mother's death from cancer, I was basically a pile of muscles and bones. Barely functional. I hired a local therapist, and in the first session, she said, "I think MBSR could help." I'd had various touchpoints with meditation over the twenty years since my first experience sitting still at the temple back in Connecticut. Each one was valuable and nudged me along the path. The eight-week program of Mindfulness-Based Stress Reduction, created by the legendary scientist/meditator/yogi Jon Kabat-Zinn, was so simple in essence. And it got me out of the house, alone, once a week which may have been what I really needed. I have since taken a second MBSR eight-week course, during another low-energy dark period, and have imperfectly managed a meditation practice ever since.

> *I dreamed about my first morning in India. From my bed in Mumbai, I looked out the open window and the sky was white. I blinked a few times, expecting the color to change. The buildings were also white, though stained under each apartment window with long drips of pollution. Far below my fifth-floor view, I saw groups of Indian women buzzing around shopping, talking, and mothering. The bright, deep colors of their saris shimmered as the sequins, tiny mirrors, and gold thread caught the sunlight. I let out a slow and audible exhalation and marveled at the contrast.*

At Home Within, a.k.a. Self-Acceptance

Once I was finally able to cobble together meaningful savings for the first time in my life, I planned a six-month trip to Southeast Asia and India by myself—a spiritual walkabout of sorts. For me, it took letting go of everything I had, saying goodbye to my family and friends, resigning from my teaching job, putting everything in storage, giving up my apartment in San Francisco, and traveling overseas to learn three simple lessons: remember to breathe, follow your heart, and be grateful. And that is where I received the gift of true and lasting gratitude on a cellular level. How I got there was totally unexpected.

I was riding a chairlift at Alpine Meadows Ski Resort in Lake Tahoe with my friend Shane, taking in the view of the blue water and white-capped mountains. Wiping the snow off his goggles, he asked, "Carrie, what would you do if you had ten years to live?" Startled, but intrigued by the question, I immediately answered, "I would get married and have one to three children. Oh, or I would travel the world for six months of each year and spend the other six months with family and friends." There I was, twenty-nine and single, wanting more than anything to create a family, but also having a deep desire to travel and see the world. I already knew I could not manifest the man on demand, but I realized I could go abroad. On that chairlift, I had woken up to a lost dream and remembered my soul's desire to explore the world and experience new people, places, and things. It helped that Shane was a world traveler himself, and we spent the rest of the weekend brainstorming where I wanted to go, when I would leave, and what it would take to get there. I was opening to this possibility, and part of me thought I might even meet *the guy* while traveling.

A week later, I gave notice that I wasn't coming back for the following school year at my teaching job in San Francisco. And so began six months of preparation for my journey to Asia. It was not only the intricacies of Asian culture, the architecture of Buddhist temples, and the simple, contemplative beauty of Buddhas themselves that drew me in, but I loved Asian food. I had wanted to travel to Asia ten years prior after graduating with a bachelor's degree in religion, but I became distracted by moving to California and starting a teaching career.

I told my parents, and they panicked, expressing fear for my finances, career, and safety. They did not know anyone who had traveled where I was planning to go. After reminding them I had traveled alone before, for two months around Australia, after a semester abroad in Melbourne, they nodded with forced smiles, and my mom mustered, "You'll be back for Christmas, right?"

Then began the quintessential silent treatment from my mom, which lasted several months. I now know "freezing" like she did is a trauma response. Regardless, I knew I could do it. I derived some pleasure when other people responded to my announcement with, "What? Where? Why? You're going alone? I could never do that!" The most common question was, "What will you do when you get back?" It felt like crabs pinching onto my legs from the bottom of the sand bucket while I was trying to get out. I responded, "That's the whole point. I don't know yet!"

Celebrating my first August without a teaching job, I attended Burning Man, where my heart and mind were blasted open with beauty, creativity, inspiration, adventure, and a sense that anything was possible. After camping in the dust, losing all sense of time, experiencing deep community, and dancing under the stars for a week, I was utterly blissed out. I felt truly happy, aligned, and content. I was ready for the big departure.

Amanda, a close friend in San Francisco, had lived and worked in Bangkok for a year. She was my biggest cheerleader, and when I shared some of the negative feedback, she assured me, *Traveling in Thailand is like going to camp. It's really easy.* She offered numerous tips on where to go, where to stay when I arrived, and some Thai basics: *sa-wat-dee-ka* (how women say hello) and *kop-koon-ka* (how women say thank you). The week before I left, she took me out for dinner to Yamo, a Burmese restaurant in the Mission that had just two tables. "You are going to love it. I am so happy for you!" she exclaimed. My plan was to use Bangkok as a home base for visiting the rest of

Thailand, Cambodia, Vietnam, and Laos. As my departure date approached, I made up a three-month itinerary to appease my parents. I knew my preparations would get me to Asia; the rest was going to be otherworldly.

Shortly after I arrived overseas, I could not stop thinking about India. While traveling, I maintained appointments with my soul through daily twenty-minute sitting meditations. I also set up a simple altar wherever I was with a mini bronze Buddha and a spiritual daily reader book. Behind my closed eyes, I kept seeing images of what I thought India would look like, and I felt a strong pull. Other backpackers I synced up with shared inspiring stories about their adventures in India, and I felt *the call.* I had recently completed the yoga teacher training program, and the thought of practicing yoga in its country of origin absolutely lit me up. Though curiosity alone could have drawn me to India, it was a no-brainer when I realized how geographically close I was. I extended my trip by another three months. Even though I missed Christmas back in the States, I had to experience India for myself.

On my last day in Thailand, I met an American woman in a cooking class. Before I caught my flight to Mumbai, she insisted that I meet her friend Anne, who had taken some ten trips to India, including spending three years living in an ashram. I walked into their hotel room and was surprised to find a sixty-year-old woman asleep. My cooking buddy woke her up, and Anne took her time, slowly sitting up and slipping on her round, horn-rimmed glasses. She remained halfway under the sheets for the duration of our chat. Her silvery, straight, shoulder-length hair was pulled back on one side with a bobby pin. Anne looked at me deeply and warned, *Never let your guard down. India always wins. Watch yourself in the streets;*

it's functional chaos. About the homeless, you can't give them all money, but you can always give them your heart. Practice breathing deeply. Let India seep into your pores and appreciate your experience. Remember, in case anything happens in southern India, go to the Apollo Hospital—it's for Westerners, it's clean, and they speak English. She dismissed me by placing her hands together in front of her heart and bowing her head. *Namaste.* From my infinite heart to your infinite heart. I honor the place in you of peace, light, and truth. I honor the Universe within. I bowed in response, walked outside, and headed for the airport. My body buzzed and my mind swirled with the unknown of tomorrow: India's beauty, poverty, myths, and magic.

On my first morning in Mumbai, I awoke to the searing sound of a concrete chainsaw, and forgot where I was. I chose to fly into Mumbai because I had heard that southern India was more relaxed, liberal, and because I had one connection there. My mind flashed to the night before and reviewed what I had seen out the window of the mosquito-infested taxicab. After arriving at midnight, the side of the highway between the Mumbai airport and Colaba, the tourist district, was lined with hundreds of homeless people. Each person slept under his or her own dirty white sheet. To my American eyes, they looked like corpses. The taxi dropped me off at the Taj Mahal Hotel, and Ankur, the one person I knew on the subcontinent of India, walked me a couple of blocks to a tall apartment building with an unlit door. He was a friend of my sister's friend, which, in India, qualifies you as family, and it was all I had in that moment. We took a rickety birdcage elevator up several flights. He had arranged for me to stay in a tiny flat. This perfect stranger had been unbelievably generous and helpful to me. I felt secure knowing I had landed somewhere vetted and safe.

Needless to say, it was rustic! The "shower" consisted of a bucket of cold water with a cup, and I had to brush my teeth with bottled water. Backpackers had told me, *Avoid getting sick—never drink the water*! Ankur picked me up and bought what he described as *mostly clean food* from the neighborhood's best street vendor. Linking our elbows, he suggested, *Let's get some pan.* As we navigated the packed sidewalks, I felt relieved to be with a local. Ankur's mere presence made me less susceptible to the endless requests: "Madam, look, come inside! Like something? Scarves, shoes, cigarettes? Fifty rupees!"

We watched the pan man, with his chocolate-brown skin and a white beard, deliberately lay out several chewable heart-shaped leaves. He used his fingers like a child with paint and spread brown and then red pastes, dancing his hands through the air as fast as a drummer. He added a few pinches and sprinkles of mint, spices, seeds, gummy and crunchy things from dull silver canisters that made a *sffft, sffft* sound when he opened and closed them. Ankur instructed me in his British English, "Carrie, you must take the entire thing in one bite." Oh my God! It took me several minutes to recover from the inaugural monsoon of textures and bitter tastes exploding in the cauldron of my mouth.

Anne and other travelers had told me that India is another world, unlike anything you have ever seen or imagined before. The extreme poverty, filth, and chaos started hitting me as I toured the area by foot over the next several days. I had never conceived of people living as severely handicapped as one teenage boy I saw who walked on all fours. His hips were the highest point on his body. He put his hands up on the ledge of an outdoor restaurant, lifted himself up, and begged for food. I bought fruit from a street vendor while several flies were eating the sleep from the corners of his daughter's eyes. Children played soccer on the neighborhood garbage heap with an empty milk carton, laughing and screaming with joy. I heard stories about homeless families intentionally breaking their children's bones, so they could have more leverage to beg. In Mumbai, I saw the same girl every time I walked in or out of my flat. Her legs were deformed and broken. She walked with her hands too, but while dragging her lower body across the ground, clearing a path free from dirt and debris with her abdomen. I had to be alert and mindful at all times to avoid colliding with the seated leper reaching for my leg again, or any number of rickshaws, cockroaches, frogs, cows, buffalo, horses, monkeys, camels, elephants, motorbikes, bicycles, rats, cats, dogs, or children at any given time. *Functional chaos.*

I traveled from Mumbai to Pune by public bus in search of the yoga center originally established by *Yogacharya* B. K. S. Iyengar. Iyengar yoga was the style of yoga I had become certified to teach, and I was thrilled with this opportunity. At the first rest stop on the overnight bus journey, I learned the bus hadn't stopped where I was supposed to get off—100 km ago. The consolation prize was a drop-off *somewhere else*. I waited at a small town bus station for several hours. I sat on my backpack and read *The God of Small Things* by Arundhati Roy. A homeless boy, about six years old, caught my eye repeatedly. The whites of his eyes were a sickly yellow. *You can't give them all money, but you can always give your heart.* I started reading my book to him. The paragraph I was on described the scene at a bus station in Cochin, a town farther south. The boy started to relax, and the hand he urgently held open for money or food fell limp by his side. This quiet moment ended when his mother slapped him, yelled at him, and dragged him away.

When the bus appeared, a hysterical rush of people surrounded it and started emphatically tossing bags, rags, and even women through the windows. You had to sprint and force yourself through the crowd for a spot on the bus. After watching this scene in awe three more times in the subsequent hours, I somehow managed to squeeze my body and bag onto a bus headed in the right direction. Aboard, two different Indian families offered me fruit. I shared a three-person seat with four other people. Every few minutes, during the long, sharp turns, a man standing in the aisle above me pressed his crotch deeply into my shoulder. I felt repulsed and suffocated.

Two weeks into my journey in India, and four months after leaving San Francisco, it was Christmas night. After eating tandoori chicken at an open-air, roadside restaurant with some fellow travelers, I felt happy. I waited in line at a phone café so I could call around the US and talk to all eleven members of my immediate family. From Grosse Pointe, Michigan, my seven-year-old niece, Kate, said, "I got a yellow polka-dot horse!" From Newport, Rhode Island, my six-year-old nephew, Karl, told me, "Santa gave Char-Char a new rainbow-colored collar." Their words pierced my heart. I missed them, my siblings, my parents, my friends, and all of my nieces and nephews. I had never felt such a deep longing to be with my family, perhaps in my entire life. After we hung up, I called a girlfriend in San Francisco and, immersed in grief, let the tears flow for a while.

The next public bus I rode was windowless; they had been knocked out. The intense breeze helped alleviate the stench of human sweat on another sweltering day. The roads were too narrow for opposing traffic and the bus frequently veered off the pavement, grazing trees and leaving a flurry of leaves and dust, as well as scratch marks, on passengers. In one hazy, exhausted moment, far ahead on the road, I saw something bright yellow and glowing at the edge of a dark-green forest. Six beautiful Indian women came into focus, dressed in matching yellow saris, with yards of loose fabric flowing behind them.

People stared at me constantly on the bus. I could feel them watching and studying me. They strained their necks to read my journals and listened intently whenever I spoke. It was unnerving but understandable, since I was a pale, white-blond, blue-eyed foreigner. The customary dress code and energy of suppressed sexuality compounded this uncomfortable feeling. I often felt constricted, choked, and stifled under my long, loose shoulder and leg coverings. I did not feel like myself.

More often than not, when I answered a question from an Indian man, I felt entangled. "Which country? American? Name? Profession? Religion? Looking for husband?" I refused a few marriage proposals along the way. Once, a young girl matched my pace as I was walking and started asking me questions. Moments later, I was surrounded by a pack of gypsy children tugging and pulling at my clothes, bag, and hands. I dashed through them and into a jewelry store. The shopkeeper yelled at the children in Hindi, and they scattered in different directions. *Never let your guard down.* I rented a bicycle for a few days in Cochin, a fishing town, and felt like a child set loose on the neighborhood for the first time; it was incredibly liberating and empowering to zoom past the groups of lurkers, some in loincloths and some in regular clothes. In other moments, locals were incredibly gracious, offering me seats, directly answering questions, helping me with my luggage, and murmuring, "*Ssst, ssst,*" reminding me when to get on or off the train.

Amma's Amritapuri Ashram in Kollam, Kerala, sat in a coconut grove and was only accessible by boat from backwaters along the Arabian Sea. It offered cheap rooms to travelers in exchange for chores—*seva.* I was assigned to clean toilets throughout the property. My only roommate was a giant flying cockroach. The insect was terrifying in size, and when I walked closer, it buzzed toward me, but never out the door. This creature escorted me through two nights of nightmares before I finally caught it in a saucepan on my third day there. On that Sunday, along with ten thousand other people, I waited in line for *darshan*, a hugging embrace, from Saint Amma. This modern-day guru's message is about love, service, and knowing who we truly are. Her congregation claims the miraculous power of her hugs—from nagging questions becoming answered to otherwise inexplicable recoveries from terminal diseases. I wanted to know what her hug felt like, what I would feel, and if I too would be *changed.*

I sat in line for half a day, dizzy from thirst and hunger and intoxicated by the reverberating live Hindu chanting. Then, it was my turn. I was ushered to the stage by her handlers and knelt at her feet like everyone else before me had. She looked into my eyes, pulled me close into her breast, mumbled a blessing in Hindi, and then let go. It's true that I felt a kind of illuminating impact of her jasmine-scented hug for a few minutes afterward. Outside, however, my mind resumed its normal activity of self-concern: how I would spend my afternoon, when and where my next meal would come from, and which town I was headed to tomorrow....

Before I took my first overnight train, a rickshaw driver parked me near a herd of cows and the neighborhood trash heap. He dashed into a shop to buy a chain for my luggage, rumored to be a "good deterrent." I looked around and saw a man walking his bicycle with what looked like a leaf blower duct taped to the seat. The machine blasted large quantities of thick gray smoke, which caused all the children in sight to run elsewhere. Sitting in that rickshaw, I smelled the most sublime masala and the most rancid, rotten garbage in the same breath. *Take time to breathe it in.*

On the train that night, the male-to-female ratio was about twenty-five-to-one. I made friends with a male Indian college student, Sudheesh, who spoke fluent English and loved to talk. During our last rest stop, he took me past the jeans and fried dough stand for *upid*, a warm, wet, spicy cornmeal snack served in a banana leaf and wrapped in newspaper. After this midnight snack, I climbed up to my bunk, a piece of metal covered with dirty blue rubber hanging from the ceiling. I brushed a cockroach and dust aside and snuggled up with my small backpack of valuables (camera, passport, cash) clutched in my arms. The symphony of snores began at once and Sudheesh, on the opposite top bunk, and I could not stop giggling. Our berth was at the end of the train, and every time a passenger opened the toilet, we inhaled a strong breeze of mixed pee. Several hours later after a restless sleep, I too felt a dull ache in my bladder and heard, "Coffee, coffee, coffeeeee" getting louder and louder as the coffee man lugged his jug down the length of the train. The sun was rising, indicating it was time to switch trains.

I almost boarded the wrong train and stood by three different tracks before making it onto the Bangalore-Mysore Express. After walking up and down the right train several times, following misinformation and mixed messages, I discovered the cabin listed on my ticket—#S11—did not exist. I was trying to follow the rules, to find my assigned seat, to say, "I belong here." Unable to move, I slumped down onto my backpack in the standing-room-only area outside the bathroom, overwhelmed and exhausted beyond imagination. A big cry moved up through my belly, into my throat, and burned my eyes when a two-year-old Indian girl began talking to me in *God only knows* what language. She stared into my eyes and leaned in close to my face. She kept smiling and laughing hysterically. After her dad bought me some, "Chai, chai, chaiiiii," the child ended up napping in my arms for two hours with her parents' loving and grateful permission. I remembered the healing power of children and missed my first-grade students more than I thought I would.

That night I decided to meditate
editate
ditate
itate
tate
ate
te
e
and warm tears streamed
down my cheeks
until I fell asleep.

Meg, the owner of my yoga studio back in San Francisco, suggested that I head to the Indus Valley Ayurvedic Center in Mysore: "Trust me, you'll need it." The center specializes in authentic ayurvedic treatments: detoxes, oil baths and massages, raw foods, and packages for rejuvenation. My reservation was for one night, two days, and three treatments. I felt ecstatic to have my own quiet room with a soft double bed, clean white sheets *on the top and bottom*, a private bathroom with a Western toilet, and a piping hot shower. Within minutes, I fell asleep for three delicious hours. I had arrived sick, and for the remainder of my time at the Center, I was sentenced to a liquids-only diet, which they delivered to my door. I nodded off between bites of boiled apple. My upset stomach got worse—much worse—after my massage. Two women had simultaneously kneaded me hard, fast, and deep, like a 140-pound pile of oiled dough. They put me in a steam box and later washed my hair and back as I sat on a wooden stool in the shower, totally wasted. After my session, my guide, who walked me to and from my treatments, pointed to the sky and said, "Look, madam, look!" She was looking at a plane sparkling and glowing in the sun, but I was overcome with the culmination of every thought, feeling, sensation, and experience I'd had in beautiful India. I started sobbing—I could not manage the intensity or keep it together anymore. *India always wins.*

After Indus Valley, I moved into the Sudharma House, a big, clean Indian homestay near a yoga center. They rented rooms on the top floor to Westerners for Rs. 100 ($2.50) a night. On the third day of continued stomach cramps and major digestion issues, I went to the Apollo Hospital, following Anne's suggestion. I was that American girl, with lips trembling and tears spilling out of her eyes, sitting in the all-Indian waiting room, and then I remembered to breathe. They called my name and I shook hands with the doctor. I described the previous few days and he diagnosed me with two words: "Be patient." After a series of antibiotics taken from fellow travelers, guidance from the housemother to drink young coconut milk, chanting sutras every day, practicing a few yoga postures with a legendary local instructor, reading the fifteenth book of my trip, and copious amounts of sleep, the unknown stomach virus passed and my health was restored. I felt happiness and gratitude extending throughout every cell in my body for all that India had given me, all that India had taken away, and all that India had left behind. *Let India seep into your pores and appreciate your experience.*

Despite the innumerable challenges of existing and traveling in a culture so far outside of my comfort zone, I would do it all over again. I cherished going to the post office with a motto of "*Reach Out, Throughout*" and using the stick they provided to rub glue on the back of stamps. Watching a travel agent pull a train reservation sheet from a box of incense. Swimming in Dolphin Bay and hearing the salt crackling underwater. Eating love-infused home-cooked meals, off a banana leaf with my hands, at Kumari's house in Varkala and Sudhyana's house in Mysore. Seeing another tree filled with yards of cassette tape. Reading the hit comic book, *Tinkle*. Receiving sessions of Vedic astrology, tarot cards, and being initiated into Reiki levels one and two. Dancing at the hottest nightclub in Bombay called Insomnia. I remember seeing a T-shirt across the dance floor: *Buddha ~ India's contribution to world ~ peace and higher consciousness.* Singing circles of harmony for hours with two French guitarists at the Blue Moon Café. Witnessing puja, the sacred daily ritual, in the cybercafé. Waking before sunrise to the sound of chanting soaring through the open windows.

I will never forget how much I loved the endless laughter in conversations among travelers about health, food, and digestion. Passing fields filled with feathery plumes of sugarcane. Seeing women farming while wearing long, thick, cotton nightgowns complete with white, frilly semicircles around the chest. Witnessing women standing knee-deep in a river rubbing bars of soap all over the dirty clothes and dishes. Hearing the repetitive thwack of the soaked clothes being beaten on a nearby rock—*the spin cycle*. Feeling almost comforted by the familiar smell of burning trash and frankincense. Smelling vanilla, chocolate, pepper, cloves, cardamom, and cinnamon seeping out from underneath the closed spice-shop doors. Noticing with rupees, the higher the value, the larger the note. Reading a sign that said:

<u>What's Happening This Weekend</u>
Seminars on Health Education,
Homeopathy, Parenting, and Yoga
"Change Your Attitude, Change Your Life" Course
Islam Women's Movement for Peace and Prosperity
Oneness University is offering a one-day class on
liberating people from *dukkha* (suffering)
and invoking divine presence!

My breath, the only guaranteed source of comfort in a land so far from home, became a resource for answers and an access point for reducing stress. I was, at last, At Home Within. I did not meet *the guy* while traveling, but I did learn another kind of lesson pertaining to the heart. By following my intuition, I not only accomplished what I set out to do, but I also enriched my life in many visible and invisible ways. I became a person who was now more interested in helping others than in helping herself. I never had a particular *aha* moment where I knew what to do when I got home, though I trusted that another exciting journey with unexpected gifts and challenges awaited me. On the plane back to California, I contemplated all that Southeast Asia and India had blessed me with and stripped me of emotionally and physically over the last six months. Heartbreak, loving friendship, exquisite natural beauty, health, safety, a deep sense of freedom and possibility, delectable food, ego detachment, and even painstaking spiritual lessons. Finally, after receiving the profound and permanent gift of gratitude the walkabout bestowed upon my life, I was ready to go home. *Namaste.*

> "Gratitude unlocks the fullness of life. It turns what we have into enough, and more. It turns denial into acceptance, chaos to order, confusion to clarity. It can turn a meal into a feast, a house into a home, a stranger into a friend. Gratitude makes sense of our past, brings peace for today and creates a vision for tomorrow."
>
> —Melody Beattie

The trip to Southeast Asia and India was monumental on every level: physically, spiritually, and psychologically. I was changed inside and out. I returned as a more well-integrated, self-accepting adult. The change in my relationship with Self, my essential being, did not occur overnight. It was a hard-earned result of moving to California, psychedelics, natural maturity, individual therapy, grad school, a dyslexia diagnosis, group therapy, fifteen different personal growth transformational workshops—including the School of Womanly Arts Mastery Program and yoga teacher training—a ten-day silent meditation retreat, multiple excruciating breakups, traveling abroad, lots of bodywork, an autoimmune diagnosis, an infertility journey, my intuition telling me over and over that the best is yet to come and that certain things, like having a family, were *inevitable.*

For a while there, I really did think drugs might be the path to enlightenment. I can fondly recall a very strong mushroom trip in the Baja desert. I was camping on the beach with friends on New Year's Eve. We were listening to track one, "La Fille De Pékin" by Frederick Rousseau, on the *Buddha Bar IV Dinner* album, when the hallucinations came on:

> *We watched the sun set in slow minutes followed by the star-rise in the deep blue oasis of open sky; one by one, they appeared. I felt pure joy, happiness, connection, and we blissfully, uncontrollably, laughed forever. I could hear the Palo Blanco trees drinking water from the rocky earth. The ground moved in unhurried low waves in synchrony with my own breathing. I saw the rainbow matrix in the sky, now a darker royal blue, the magic and infinite grid of perfection behind the sober eye of logic and labels and ego. We walked to the water's edge and the smooth, wet, dark pebbles formed thousands of perfect, intricate swirls like a vast field of poppies tucked in for the night. My fingertips glowed with light from the stars. It was so fucking beautiful, raw, and real…*

Fyodor Dostoevsky, the 19th century Russian writer, wrote about a state of pure ecstasy uncannily similar to what I experienced on psychedelics. Apparently in his personal letters, Dostoevsky described profound changes in his perception just moments before a seizure. "For several instants, I experience a happiness that is impossible in an ordinary state, and which other people have no conception. I feel full harmony in myself, and in the whole world, and the feeling is so strong and sweet that for a few seconds of such bliss one could give up ten years of life, perhaps all of life. I felt that heaven descended to earth and swallowed me. I really attained God and was imbued with Him." Dostoevsky will long be remembered for acknowledging the irrefutable connection between suffering and spiritual insight. Mind-altering substances and psychedelic experiences undeniably shaped me as a person, but the temporary jaunts to other dimensions didn't give me the hard, cold lessons I needed to truly grow up.

Somewhere along the way, mostly witnessing older, wiser women not only function and succeed in their daily lives but also exude contentment and even happiness, I learned how to practice self-care and self-acceptance. It started with drinking water, giving myself eight hours of sleep every night, hours of screen-free time every day, plenty of exercise, and learning how to eat properly with nutrient-dense food. From there, I lived alone for the first time and reconnected with nature. In community, I practiced meditating as well as processing intense feelings and life's daily challenges. I started setting healthy boundaries and managing my meager tutoring salary without bouncing checks or overdrawing my account. I learned to WAIT: Why Am I Talking?

Today, as I write this, I feel gratitude for all of the emotional turning points in my life. I can even celebrate the sum of my inner work and the gifts I received from my personal development journey, as difficult as it was. I see how far I've come. For so long, I avoided being in my own skin, a.k.a. telling the truth. And just for today, self-care looks like leaving my children, husband, puppy, and live-in mother-in-law at home and being truly alone. I'm taking a break from my working-mother multigenerational life to retreat and feel and remember and integrate. I am writing to the soundtrack of ocean waves at my friend Paula's glorious beachfront condo. How lucky am I?!

Chapter Four

Relationships + Family Life

Throughout my career as a financial coach, my dad has often said, "I wish I could have hired a money coach for you and your siblings when you graduated from college." He's right. I definitely could have used that, however, therapy, coaching, and conversations about *healing* and *human potential* were foreign concepts in our small Midwestern town.

Couple's Money Love

We will all face challenges in adulthood. No one remains unscathed by big events like partnership, moving, job transitions, inheritance (or lack thereof), debt, health issues, and aging. And for those who choose to have children, welcome to the great catastrophe! Raising children will push all of your buttons and test and stretch you, your partner, and your relationship to limits never before explored. It's exhausting, expensive, and stressful. And becoming a mom is the best decision I've ever made. It's the hardest, best job in the world and making babies—well, everything about fertility and parenthood—is an epic journey. It took me three natural pregnancies and four rounds of IVF to have two children. That wasn't the plan, but it's what happened! And it's miraculous and I'm totally blessed with how my spirit babies came into existence. Parents also have to accept that their children will eventually develop their own unique relationship with money. For me, I knew I had to get right with money before a healthy financial partnership would be possible. I needed to become fully self-supporting and stable in my financial life. No more chaos. For better or for worse, some people pair up young and grow up financially with their partner. They fumble through early adulthood side by side while figuring out their careers, navigating paying bills, housing choices, possibly sharing money, and managing their envisioned lifestyles, values, and goals.

As I have shared, I squandered years of my life forcing square pegs into round holes in the relationship department. To save time and energy and release some of the pressure I felt and put on others, I really could have used a script of what to ask, what to share, and what to know when dating and falling in love.

Financial Partnership Questions

Getting to Know You

1. How much do you earn? Gross (grand total before taxes and deductions including bonuses) and what

is your net monthly take-home pay (after taxes and deductions)?

2. How much debt do you have? This includes student loans, personal loans, business loans, mortgages, car loans, tax debt, credit card debt, medical debt, anything in collections, and so forth. What does debt mean to you?
3. How do you use credit cards?
4. Have you ever declared bankruptcy?
5. What is your current net worth?
6. Do your parents, employers, or other people pay any of your current bills?
7. Do you currently support your parents or anticipate that you will in the future? Siblings? Charity? Others?
8. How much do you think vacations should cost?
9. What is your philosophy towards gifts for birthdays, holidays and anniversaries?
10. Are you planning to go back to school in the future? Would you take out loans?
11. Are you open to relationship money meetings?
12. Would you consider financial counseling if we decided we need it?

Family Planning

1. Do you envision we'll share a joint checking account or keep our money separate?
2. If we were to merge money, who would oversee paying our bills? Investing for the long term?
3. What is the maximum I could spend on something before consulting you?

4. How much do you think we should spend on our wedding? What's your vision for our honeymoon?
5. How many kids do you want to have?
6. How much are you willing to spend on fertility treatments or adoption if we have trouble conceiving?
7. What do you envision childcare will look like?
8. Do you want our kids to go to public or private school?
9. What are your thoughts on paying for our children's college education?
10. What would it look like if one of us stopped working when we had kids?

Values, Family History, and the Future

1. What is your earliest money memory?
2. What is your most joyful money memory?
3. What is your most painful memory of money?
4. What was the socioeconomic status of your family of origin? How did this impact your relationship with money?
5. Does your family operate as an independent or interdependent system?
6. What was the original socioeconomic status of your parents growing up?
7. Name three things you learned from your mom and three things you learned from your dad about money, either directly or indirectly.
8. What are your financial goals?
9. Are you expecting a wealth event of any kind in the future (inheritance, access to a trust, selling a company, or the like)?
10. What are your biggest financial fears?
11. What are your core values?

Additional Important Topics for Healthy Relationships

Name one thing you're willing to examine or do differently to improve our relationship. Are there more?

Name three things you appreciate or admire about your partner. Can we practice gratitude and acknowledgment routines together?

Other juicy conversations include: parenting/discipline styles, religion and what beliefs will be instilled into your children, how to deal with family members, childhood traumas, sexual expectations, partner expectations, family physical and mental health history, partner physical and mental health history, bucket lists, dream home, career goals, political views, and whatever else comes to mind!

You can download the Financial Partnership Questions at sfmoneycoach.com/downloads.

In my personal and professional experience, financial difficulty and relationship issues are circularly linked. There are many factors that can affect how we show up around money, like age, attitudes, family history, money scripts, marital quality, power and control dynamics, and mental health. Plus it is quite rare for *both* partners to enter a relationship with the same level of self-awareness or personal development experience. You can expect there will be work to do, and it's very common to struggle with making agreements at your kitchen table. And, unexpressed expectations are akin to premeditated resentments. The smartest and bravest among us reach out for help when needed.

The Law of Attraction

"Work in the invisible world at least
as hard as you work in the visible."
—Rumi

My first academic exposure to the Law of Attraction, or *oneness*, was in college. I took courses for my major about the human experience in Christianity, Taoism, Hinduism, Buddhism, Judaism, and Islam (including Sufism). We studied oral traditions, scriptures, art, material culture, beliefs, rituals, and religious institutions. I was finally reading about and studying something that I had felt intuitively my whole life: *everything is connected*. I believe we're interdependent beings in an intimate relationship with nature. And there are plenty of stories based in religion related to the power of perception, history, literature, philosophy, science, and economics to this effect.

The next confirmation of the Law of Attraction was in a film called *What the Bleep?!: Down the Rabbit Hole*, a fascinating docudrama about the intersection of spirituality, brain science, and human consciousness. I probably watched the film ten times. Back in a time before streaming, I bought the DVD and gave it away as gifts to many different family members and friends, sparking expansive conversations all around me. I was particularly into the theory that thought creates reality. In therapy at the time, I was learning the concept of taking responsibility for my life exactly the way it was and exactly the way it wasn't, and it all felt very serendipitous. In the film, scientists and spiritual leaders document and depict what happens to the brain, and water molecules, when a person thinks positive, loving, caring thoughts about it versus negativity, hatred, and vitriol. I had plenty of evidence in my own life for how I felt about myself and who I attracted when exuding self-hatred, reeking like cigarette smoke and a negative mindset. I also knew the power of psyching myself up to win an important point in tennis and that my positive self-talk worked in my favor most of the time.

In the film, Dr. Masaru Emoto performed an experiement on water molecules. The results were completely mind-blowing. He wanted to know if human thoughts and emotions had any impact on water. When people spoke loving thoughts like "peace" and "gratitude" and "thank you" to a jar of water, the water molecules formed beautiful, symmetrical shapes. Conversely, when people yelled words like "evil" and "you disgust me" at a water jar, the water molecules changed into tighter, asymmetrical shapes. My takeaway was that if water has memory and, even temporarily, stores emotion, what I say to myself and what gets stored in the cells of my body *really does matter.*

Around this time, I started reading Julia Cameron's book, *The Artist's Way: A Spiritual Path to Higher Creativity*. I joined a local "playgroup" studying her book, and we all committed to weekly artist dates like going to an art museum, window shopping to explore textures, drawing in nature, or seeing live music. As a group, we built forts, painted, danced, and did laughing yoga. But it was the "morning pages" that really *opened the channel* for me. The core practice in the book is daily journaling with the instructions: keep the pen moving without judgment, write for yourself (not an audience), and just enjoy the stream of consciousness. It didn't

"Look around less. Imagine more… The entire Universe is conspiring to give you everything that you want… Believe in what you want so much it has no choice but to materialize… Everything That Is, is the result of vibration. And if you don't like the result, change the vibration!"

—Abraham Hicks

take long to see patterns in my thoughts, like repetitive complaints of incompatibility with men and my soul really wanting to take a big leap, like moving across the bay.

Then, I joined a weekly women's circle with some of the same ladies from the *Artist's Way* playgroup. The first night, I was given some bootleg CDs of Abraham Hicks, a group of non-physical entities channeled by a woman named Esther Hicks.

I loved this philosophy and was sold immediately, of course. I even attended an in-person workshop with Esther Hicks, a.k.a. Abraham, along with hundreds of other seekers in a hotel lobby in Monterey. Our women's circle practiced *the art of allowing* every Wednesday night for two years. We sat knee to knee in a circle on the floor of the host's apartment and shared our visions. The very act of speaking our desires aloud, in present tense, with witnesses for ten to fifteen minutes each, was very powerful. We often spoke through tears as we took turns shedding layers of unworthiness and perfectionism. Our sacred circle provided beautiful, positive, healing energy for all of us.

So, these were the types of conversations I was having in my spare time, when not working or playing tennis. In my experience, the Law of Attraction is about reimagining your reality. Go ahead and give it a try:

What do you *want* your financial life to look like? And then what?

____

____

____

____

Where do you live and what does your home look like? What else?

____

____

____

____

How many hours a week are you working? Describe your work life, colleagues, and the environment.

____

____

____

____

What do you and friends do together for fun? Tell me more!

____

____

____

____

Back in 2001, I was working on my graduate school thesis, "The Role of Technology in the Elementary Classroom Setting," and thinking about how I needed a job. I grabbed a piece of blank, white paper and jotted down in vivid detail everything I wanted:

<u>My Ideal Teaching Job</u>

Head Teacher Position in Kindergarten, First, or Second Grade

Progressive School in San Francisco

Casual Dress for Teachers
Students Call Me Carrie
Inspiring Professional Development Opportunities
Environmental Education Component

I taped the poster on the wall, and within three weeks, I had been hired at the Children's Day School in the Mission District, a perfect match with my list, to a "T"—a miracle!

Here's another example of intentional manifestation. Ever since I was a little girl, I had known deep in my bones that I wanted to be a mom.. And my vision included a committed relationship with a man. So I was living in Mill Valley at the time, recovering from a three-year relationship mired with financial abuse with an older man and his two darling toddler girls. It had been a triple, monstrous breakup and one of the most difficult emotional experiences of my life. However, this lovely man, at the eleventh hour, confessed that he did not want more children afterall. I moved out a week later. *Ugh.* When I arrived at the doorstep of my new apartment in Marin (with a creek and redwoods outside the windows), there was a stunning arrangement of white roses waiting for me. I read the card. "*Dearest Carrie, We wish you all the best in Marin and have faith that all of your dreams will come true.*" It was signed by my ex's mom and two would-have-been sisters-in-law. The power of women supporting women is astonishing.

The gift blasted my heart open into smithereens, and I literally crumpled to the floor in the hallway and sobbed. But I believed what they wrote, that becoming a mom was inevitable, even though more cards were stacking up against me: age, time, fertility, geographical location, pressure from family, and social humiliation. I spent the next year trying to change and mold a variety of men into an ideal partner and failed over and over again.

I needed a break. I was exhausted and feeling more hopeless than hopeful most days. I decided to take six months off from dating. Shocking, right? I was *that desperate*, and it turned out this contrary action was exactly what I needed to do. I closed my online dating accounts. No lunches. No flirting. Just alone time. To my surprise, after withdrawal subsided, I felt happy and uplifted again. I was in the flow with myself, busy with my new money coaching practice, and enjoying my own company. In these quiet moments, I heard an unexpected whisper in my ear. *What about New York City?* It didn't make any sense. But maybe it did. I was going on my 14th year in the Bay Area. I had friends in Manhattan from college, my hometown, and other places who had already left SF along with my beloved younger brother, Peter—a walk-in community of sorts. Maybe it would be nice to be in the same time zone as my entire family. After much deliberation, I decided if I was going to make a colossal change and move out of California, New York was the only place I would consider. So, I did it. Thirty-six, single, and self-employed. I sold my car and furniture and significantly downsized. I bought a one-way flight and landed in a summer sublet on the corner of Jane Street and 14th Avenue in the West Village. By then, I was feeling ready to date again. A short five months later, a chat window popped up from my future husband while Hurricane Sandy pummeled the city outside my fifth-story walk-up. And so, "There is no joy in owning anything unshared" met "West Village racquet sports girl seeks life partner" at Le Pain Quotidien Café on the Upper West Side. He mentioned he was from the Bay Area. "That's funny," I said. "I just moved here from there, and I'm going there for

Thanksgiving in two weeks." He was too. The Universe was winking at us. I could *feel* it. I had moved to New York, following my intuition on a hope and a prayer, and *that's where I met my California guy*. Miracle!

We were realistic and, therefore,got married one year later. I became quickly pregnant with our first child, whom I delivered back in Marin County, California, at the ripe age of thirty-nine. Just under the radar, I like to say! The relationship breakthrough came from sitting in the muck and, like a lotus flower in all its glory, I did eventually emerge as someone whole and worthy. I cannot prove that getting right with money was an ingredient in manifesting a trustworthy, solid, loving financial partnership with a good man, but deep in my heart, I knew it was all connected.

At the risk of sounding too *woo-woo,* I am suggesting you feel the vibes (vibrations) you want to feel about money. And then *act as if.* If you want to enjoy the flow of money, you need to surround yourself with people who have what you want and are already in the stream of abundance. Study their habits. Be bold and ask them questions about how to get started, what they're reading or what kind of systems and support they have in their lives. Most importantly, believe that what you seek is seeking you.

Letting Go

Before the wedding and the baby, we moved in together, and it brought up a lot of questions and feelings about money. Even though by the end of the first month in the relationship we had disclosed our money habits, salary levels, ability to sustain savings (or not), and broad strokes on our net worths, I knew we had a long way to go. I did not yet have the Financial Partnership Questions but, regardless, it was time to get organized. We were already deep in the throes of several expensive conversations: buying furniture, cosigning on a car, and, *ahem*, planning a wedding.

However, before we had the mental and physical bandwidth to sit down and take a rigorous look at our household finances, we had to merge kitchens, sort through our book collections, empty and refill our storage space, and set up my home office. I tried my best to bring an attitude of curiosity and nonjudgment when I asked him questions like, "Do you really need four spatulas?" And I made an effort to listen reverently when he explained the precise function of each one. It became obvious and necessary for both of us to let go of excess clothes, furniture, miscellaneous household items, kitchen supplies, and even superfluous trips to the grocery store. After many late nights excavating every nook and cranny of our newly shared space, at least a thousand, "Is this essential?" decision points, multiple trips to Goodwill, and, of course, a little sage-burning ritual (to cleanse the space), at last we found ourselves in our mutually acceptable, refreshed new home. Now, it was time to streamline our cash flow.

At the recommendation of my own money coach, I requested a single joint account for us to contain and organize all that was happening in our household. I would maintain a separate business account, and he was now in a position share *everything* about his financial life. This made him itch a little, and there were references to his first marriage, fear of losing independence, and questions like, "What about privacy for, um, gifts?" Between the two of us, we had sixteen bank accounts. I *knew* we needed to focus on one primary checking account for the majority of our monthly transactions.

Here's my case for a primary joint account:

Transparency
Intimacy
Fun

Transparency—We all want the same things: to see and be seen, love and be loved, and to feel connection. An agreement to be open about money requires deep conversations and recognition of what's important, what's acceptable, and what's nonnegotiable. Avoiding these topics would spell trouble for both our financial and romantic lives.

Intimacy—Pema Khandro, a Tibetan Buddhism teacher formerly known as Kali Ma, once said there are three essential components for a healthy and sustainable relationship: shared values, shared vision, and shared desire for personal growth. Money decisions exist in each these areas. If we can learn to share, discuss, and understand each other's financial needs, desires, habits, earning power, and goals, the shared financial wellness journey can be powerful, transformative, and deeply intimate.

Fun—Money is a necessary tool to generate plans and create a life of pleasure, well-being, and adventure. By paying close attention and regularly tending to our garden of money, we can align our behaviors with the reality of our collective funds *and* goals. Not only that, but we can also master the domain of personal finance and more effectively realize the fabulous lives we envision for ourselves.

Ultimately, my then fiancé agreed that sharing a joint account would be the right path, but I had to make some adjustments too. I surrendered to his request of putting everything on a credit card, something I had consciously decided not to do for the last six years. However, I negotiated for paying off the card in full on the thirtieth of every month to contain that month's spending for budgeting purposes, and for ten minutes of meditation together every day. Like I said, some things are nonnegotiable.

To reiterate, I generally recommend that most couples go all-in, or fully joint, in terms of checking accounts, credit cards, and basic cash savings. One of my colleagues won't work with couples unless they've already set up and started using their joint account. I understand there are good arguments for couples not going fully joint. When one or both people in a relationship have endured extreme situations such as abuse (sexual, emotional, spiritual, incest, abandonment, or shaming), poverty, divorce, addiction, bankruptcy, reckless spending, insurmountable debt, foreclosure, unemployment, theft, scams, bank collapse, market events, or infidelity, I would not recommend any rash decisions. People exposed to or victims of abuse or financial trauma need to be held tenderly and supported with love, understanding, and compassion.

Some of my clients have inherited strong messaging around always keeping their own bank account. This urgency usually comes from people in their own families—often women—who stayed in terrible marriages or suffered atrocities related to a lack of funds, autonomy, agency, financial literacy, transparency, or general access to money. Other times, there's no trauma; wanting to remain independent is more of a feminist expression to stand on your own two feet.

I had two clients who were considering filing for divorce around the same time. The similarities in their stories are astonishing. At first, they had access to nothing in terms of actual cash or checking accounts, only credit cards.. They both spent without limit, and their ultrawealthy husbands handled the finances. After the absolute flurry of raising two young children while buying and decorating two houses each, both women realized they didn't have a debit card or access to a checkbook—nothing in their own names. In cases like these, I recommended they immediately apply online or drive to a bank and request a checking account with one name on it. Now, funding the account was a different kind of challenge, but doable, and they both made significant requests that were met with little resistance. The essential first steps in regaining some power and turning around their financial lives were setting a boundary and asking for what they needed.

All of these arguments for separate accounts are valid, and I wholeheartedly agree that independence is important *and* keeping separate checking accounts can make planning, alignment, and communication more difficult. It is much easier to track spending, reflect, look ahead, and make decisions as a unified front when you have just one main checking account to grapple with.

Money Dates

Regardless of whether or not you combine money with your honey in a primary joint account, you need to talk about money on a regular basis. Couples get into trouble when one person, or worse, both partners, hide behind old patterns of denial, avoidance, and money fog. "I'm too busy. And, I'm exhausted.

Besides, every time we talk about money it ends in a fight." Sound familiar?

Couples that experience the most ease and deepest connection in the finance department typically meet for an hour every week, especially in the beginning. Some of my clients have called their money dates "Weekly Home Office Hours" or "Family Admin Time." Single people need money dates too, but half an hour should do it since they don't have to deal with dynamics, semantics, and someone else's *money stuff*. Remember, in a financial partnership, you're dealing with three marriages: one to self, one to work, and one to your partner. There can be a lot to sift through while setting yourself up for success, making time for money conversations, and keeping the peace.

Here are seven tips for productive and meaningful money dates:

Time is sacred.
Remember the wonders of childcare.
Be intentional with locations.
Tune in.
Be the master of the obvious.
Stay connected.
End money dates by planning the next one.

1. Your time is sacred. It's important to make an appointment for a money date with a specific time and date. Ambushing and fly-by money questions are not respectful. No, thank you! No interruptions allowed: no children, no scheduling conflicts, no cell phone, and not even work. Ideally, you would meet at the same time every week, or once a month if you've been doing this awhile. In terms of frequency, once a month is

sufficient if you can both stay connected and present throughout the talk and you have a good rhythm with the personal finance routines. If the conversations are emotionally fraught and difficult, or you have a backlog of financial housekeeping tasks to do, I recommend setting aside time every week in a kind of exposure therapy approach. The more you practice money dates, the easier they will become, and something may have to give to find time for this new healthy habit. Schedule your money dates for an optimal time. As my financial planner once told me, "No talking about money between six and nine p.m.!" It goes without saying that after nine p.m., the topic of money is off-limits.

2. <u>Childcare is available.</u> Use it, if needed—seriously!
3. <u>Choose a conducive environment</u>. Which location is best? A café, the kitchen table, your office, your friend's apartment, or somewhere else? My financial therapist instructed me, "Avoid money matters in the bedroom at all costs!"
4. <u>Check in before you start</u>. Begin with a soft start-up like, "Let's check in. How's your day going? How are you feeling?" If you find yourself at a money date feeling irritable or agitated, a quick body scan or a one-minute meditation might help. It's ideal to be equanimous, *upekkha*, and clearheaded when discussing money. Remember to HALT. Hungry? Grab some snacks and power through. If you can't get past the angry, lonely, and tired feelings, it's probably best to postpone the date until you feel better and can start from an open, positive place. My acupuncturist always reminds me to keep the big four in balance: food, water, sleep, and

stress. Self-care is critical to making money dates work. Just be sure to reschedule!

5. Practice being a master of the obvious. Many people feel overwhelmed when they sit down for a money date, as if they're opening the hallway closet overloaded with stuff. There's a fear of the avalanche. The most productive money dates are based on accurate numbers, likely from an updated financial tracking software system, and going through the personal finance routines. If you're still working on setting up your system, that should take precedence. Otherwise, look at the obvious places to start the conversation and choose *one* to start with.

    - Track Your Spending—categorize your spending, or minimally, read and integrate your bank statement
    - Monthly Spending Plan—examine the budget versus reality, make adjustments, or plan the upcoming month
    - Annual Budget—look at the monthly totals and the twelve-month plan
    - Periodic (Non-monthly) Expenses
    - Systems
    - Paperwork, Mail, and Files
    - Goals
    - Reimbursements
    - Interpersonal Dynamics
    - Any Burning (Urgent) Financial Topics

6. It's okay to take a break. If the date stops feeling productive and peaceful, take a deep breath. Acknowledge it and determine whether you need a break (short or long), a glass of water, a hug, a dance party, or perhaps

you want to talk it out or process a trigger point. When we flip our lids, the fight, flight, or freeze response takes over and the prefrontal cortex shuts down. Like it or not, it takes about twenty minutes to recover from feeling that discombobulated. And, whatever comes up comes up to be healed.

7. <u>Always wrap up a money date by planning the next one</u>. Regular money dates will not only help you make financial decisions and plans together, but these financial state-of-the-union conversations help to prevent arguments and conflicts down the road. A healthy and sustainable financial partnership can last a lifetime and, like a garden, it needs to be tended to and watered consistently.

We all know that good communication, and an ability to self-soothe and soothe the other, are all critical in any relationship. But did you know these skills are also essential to finance wellness? The skill of talking about money without emotionally or physically collapsing is crucial to maintaining a healthy financial life and getting what you want. After all, you cannot make sound decisions about your money if you're not able to express yourself, put words to the numbers, or share your feelings and desires. There's a lot to talk about between spending, saving, earning, lifestyle choices, and allocating funds within a partnership. These conversations are not easy, but they are doable even if you must *fake it 'til you make it* for a while. Money dates are intimate, and finances can become a topic you actually bond over. For a deeper dive, I highly recommend checking out the Gottman Institute. My husband and I did an intensive in-person couples retreat with the famous Julie and John Gottman at their home on Orcas Island, Washington. The workshop, itself, was both confronting and affirming, and I am so grateful for this once-in-a-lifetime experience. We were assigned to read two of their books: *The Seven Principles for Making Marriage Work: A Practical Guide from the Country's Foremost Relationship Expert* and *Fight Right: How Successful Couples Turn Conflict Into Connection*—both of which I highly recommend.

Love Languages + Money

Dr. Gary Chapman, PhD, wrote a book called *The 5 Love Languages*. He asserts that the five primary ways to express love are words of affirmation, physical touch, acts of service, quality time, and gifts. The premise is that in order to foster truly healthy and sustainable relationships, it's essential to know your own dominant love language as well as those of your partner, parents, siblings, children, and friends. This awareness can even extend into your professional life. Let's explore how each love language can affect your financial life.

Words of Affirmation—Zero dollars! Generally speaking, there is no cost to written or verbal words of affirmation on paper or a digital form. The only potential financial impact is in the delivery method. Words of Affirmation people tend to love and notice things like handmade cards or high-end, personalized stationery and, of course, you do have to pay for texts and some email services.

Touch—Completely free! Healthy affection can be a wonderful way to show people you love them by offering hugs, holding hands, snuggling, doing partner yoga, and giving massages. The potential financial impact includes special gifts like beauty treatments, spa days, retreats, and expensive clothing.

Acts of Service—Zero dollars! By the very nature of this love language, there is no actual cost associated with doing the dishes, preparing a meal, folding the laundry, making the bed, running errands, cleaning up after, or performing other random acts of kindness. If you choose to book a professional to detail a car, plan a trip for your family, or procure dinner every night for a week, that will cost you.

Quality Time—Free, but could turn costly! People who need quality time to feel loved enjoy talking, eating a meal, watching TV, playing games, working on creative projects, exercising, traveling, or any number of activities—as long as it's with you. There is a range of potential costs associated with every form of quality time, and these lifestyle and entertainment preferences are subject to your loved ones' desires and family budget.

Gifts—Uh-oh! This love language is likely the most expensive of them all. We all know these beloved gifters. They can't help themselves and not only enjoy but *need* to express or receive love through gifts. Some gifters can contain their giving or manage their expectations of receiving gifts on special occasions only. But for others, expectations are high and frequent. Overspending can be a slippery slope for folks with this love language. They buy superfluous experiences, services, and things as gifts for others simply because they express love through gifts. It is possible to slow the financial impact with communication, agreed-upon limits, and experimenting with other love languages.

How can you strike a balance with your loved ones? You must first be aware of your own love language and then be curious about your beloved's love language. Some people prefer to give one way and receive another. This is complicated stuff!

Giving Contest

Within twenty-four hours of joining our individual checking accounts, my fiancé bought the top item on his wish list: new golf clubs. I was happy he got what he wanted, but I'd be lying if I said it didn't touch a nerve. I took a few deep breaths and let it go.

About a week later, he came home with a huge, heavy box in his arms. "It's a telescope for our trip to Colorado! Maybe we can give it to your brother-in-law when we get back." A $500 gift for no apparent reason? I couldn't tell if these spontaneous purchases were somehow connected to our newly mutual funds. Was this some sort of test, and was I passing?

As I thought about it some more, I wasn't concerned about whether we had enough money for those items. We did, and if they were necessary right then, so be it. Rather, I realized that his purchases caused stress for me because I don't like surprises and I am a terrible gift giver. I was learning that the ideal of a neat spending plan may not always be possible in the context of a joint account. For instance, if I kept current with our expenses the way I'd like to and did as a single person, we'd be talking about money every single day. In this new arrangement of cohabitation and partnership, however, I would have to be patient. There is a time and place for nitty-gritty money conversations with your partner, but it's not appropriate or fun to enforce daily financial talks. I swore to myself I would not be like my father, cringing at the report or sight of every purchase made by "the other" or judging my partner's love of and need to give gifts. True emergencies aside, I needed to simply wait for our midmonth money date.

In doing so, I discovered that one of my fiancé's core values, perhaps his dominant love language, was gifting. He is very generous and thoughtful in that area. I, on the other hand, have childhood trauma around receiving gifts on holidays and special occasions. In my family, gifts often triggered fighting and yelling and my dad marching off to go back to work on Christmas, on my birthday, and on my graduation day. Still to this day, I find giving and receiving gifts incredibly awkward. It's an area of great weakness and insecurity, so it's no wonder I didn't understand what Andrew was doing. Clearly, I was starting to discover the art of compromise in marriage.

On the spender-saver spectrum, I think you can guess by now that in the context of shared family finances, I definitely lean toward saving and financial security. This was a shift for me that came along with domesticity. I know now that his choices were not tests; he was just being himself. And when I took a reality check on what happened that month, I realized that I spent a good amount of discretionary money too. In fact, there was the time he picked me up at my favorite clothing store on the Upper East Side, Comptoir Des Cotonniers, and I asked him to wait outside while my purchases were tallied. Personal finance is a sensitive, nuanced area in relationships, and if either or both of us react *unconsciously,* we not only risk disconnection, but we're laying the groundwork for future fights about money.

In the end, rather than insisting on a detailed dialogue about my fiancé's thought process before, during, and after the golf clubs and telescope purchases, I let nature take care of things. The thick, high-altitude clouds prevented him from viewing the Dumbbell Nebula on any of our four nights in southwest Colorado, and he chose to return the telescope for a full refund. I never said anything, and it turns out my fear and anxiety were unfounded. Ultimately, I was reminded that sharing money is about unconditional love, and that the most successful relationships accept what they are truly in contract for: a giving contest.

Young Children + Money

It happened overnight. My eight-year-old daughter woke up with a lot of questions. "How much money do you have? How much money do *I* have? How can I get more money? What do I do with my money?" So began the conversations around regular chores, extra paid chores, allowance, and bank accounts. Researchers have identified the importance of early learning in the areas of consumption, spending, and saving in age-appropriate ways, but honestly, I made it up as I went along. Here's what worked.

We started by counting the coins in her turtle bank. As a second grader, she had learned the basics about money at school and could accurately count coins and do some mental math. Right away, I ordered her (and her best friend) a "money jars" system from Etsy, with containers for Save, Give, Invest, and Spend. (Visit sfmoneycoach.com/resources for my favorite.) I firmly believe kids learn best by touching real-world materials, not from watching a screen. We took her coins to the grocery store and got some bills for them. We came home and she asked:

"Well, which jar do I put them in?"

Me: "Is there anything you want to spend it on right now?"

"Candy!"

Me: "Okay, great, put some money in Spend."

"I'll put the rest in Save."

Me: "Oh! Do you have something in mind you're saving money for?"

"No, but wait. What does Invest mean?"

Me: "Investing is a special kind of savings account where you buy a share in a company that you like. It's important that you believe in the company's success! When you invest money, you typically don't touch it again for a long time and, hopefully, it compounds or grows and grows.

"Okay, I definitely want to do that! I want a million dollars! What is Give for?"

Me: "Some people like to give money to charities and nonprofits and people in need, like children without toys."

She silently put some money in Give. I could tell she was thinking deeply about this.

Unexpectedly, the seeds I had planted that day about giving led to a significant baking project where she raised eighty dollars for a local nonprofit that provides basic services like showers, new clothing, and interview practice for the unhoused. Lucy also kept eighty dollars—exactly half the profit. That was her choice, and even though her grandmother shook her head and thought that Lucy should donate all of it, I was proud of her. She had worked hard on the project even with school, homework, and acting in sixteen *Nutcracker* performances around that same time.

Next, we had to face a conversation about chores. Some parents believe kids should never get paid for household responsibilities and that pitching in is part of being in a family. Either way, parents have a significant impact on the financial behavior of their children. I understood my responsibility, *and* when I looked more closely, I saw how much Lucy already does and that her jobs around the house have naturally increased as she's gotten older. Also, I believe there are opportunities for meaningful paid work at home. We talked about all the ways in which she takes care of our home. And we brainstormed a new list of "more intense" chores—ones that take longer, are a bit less fun, and are not exactly easy. Ones where she might get dirty and extra effort is involved. There's no right or wrong way to parent or to set up work charts or give money to your children. Every family has their own set of values around chores and allowance and I give you permission to navigate this topic in your own way. If you need help getting started or knowing what's generally age-appropriate, check out this chore chart:

Ages 2–3

- Put toys away.
- Stack books on shelf.
- Place dirty clothes in laundry hamper.
- Throw trash away.
- Carry firewood.
- Fold washcloths.
- Set the table.
- Fetch diapers and wipes.
- Dust baseboards.

Ages 4–5

- Feed pets.
- Wipe up spills.

- Make the bed.
- Straighten up the bedroom.
- Water houseplants.
- Sort clean silverware.
- Prepare simple snacks.
- Use the handheld vacuum.
- Clear kitchen table.
- Dry and put away dishes.
- Disinfect doorknobs.

Ages 6–7

- Gather trash.
- Fold towels.
- Sweep and mop floors.
- Empty most of the dishwasher.
- Match clean socks.
- Weed garden.
- Rake leaves.
- Peel potatoes or carrots.
- Make salad.
- Replace toilet paper rolls.

Ages 8–9

- Load the dishwasher.
- Change light bulbs.
- Wash laundry.
- Fold clean clothes and put them away.
- Dust furniture.
- Spray off the patio.
- Put groceries away.
- Scramble eggs.

- Bake cookies.
- Walk the dogs.
- Sweep the porches.
- Wipe off the table.

Ages 10–11

- Clean bathrooms.
- Vacuum rugs.
- Clean countertops.
- Deep clean the kitchen.
- Prepare a simple meal.
- Mow the lawn.
- Bring in mail.
- Do simple mending.
- Sweep out the garage.

Ages 12 and up

- Mop the floors.
- Change overhead lights.
- Wash and vacuum the car.
- Trim hedges.
- Paint walls.
- Shop for groceries with a list.
- Cook a complete dinner.
- Bake bread or dessert.
- Do simple home repairs.
- Wash windows.
- Iron clothes.
- Watch younger siblings.

If you're anything like me, when I read that list, I realized I do too much and I've got to let my kids help more! I appreciated the reminder of just how capable children of all ages can be. The Age-Appropriate Children's Chore Chart is reprinted with permission from the Flanders family and is available to download at sfmoneycoach.com/downloads.

Lastly, regarding bank accounts, at first I opened a kids' savings account for my daughter at our primary bank. I was able to show her the modest starting balance online, but she quickly forgot about it. Her actual coins and bills, mostly ones plus a couple of fives and a twenty, really captured her attention. A few years later, I switched to Greenlight which ties chore tracking to allowance. Greenlight comes with a customizable debit card, opportunities to allocate money for spending, saving, giving and investing, basic financial education infotainment videos and the app is super easy for parents to use. I feel excited about guiding my kids' financial wellness journeys and to witness their future money-related decisions. And, my intention is for my children to use real paper cash as much as possible well into their teenage years since I strongly believe cash is the best teaching tool.

Lucy's little brother, Max, was paying attention to all of this money talk too. At the age of four, I caught him and his friend sneaking into her room, taking some of Lucy's money, and stuffing it into their pockets. I nonchalantly set a boundary, took it back, returned the funds, and put her money jars out of sight and reach of the little ones. I wonder if *being caught* will be Max's first financial flashpoint, a.k.a. memory with money. Only time will tell! Go to sfmoneycoach.com/resources for more on chores, conscious parenting, and moneywise kids.

A Prescription for Teens + Young Adults

When I was in my early twenties, I was fully winging the money thing. I had not received any comprehensive instruction on the ABCs or 123s of personal finance, and I felt like I had no one to talk to. This resulted in quickly accumulating credit card debt, building up huge emotions about money, and being internally flattened by overwhelming shame. I originally compiled the following financial education for parents of teens and young adults for a private financial wellness workshop. One of my favorite colleagues who later became a client, a marriage and family therapist herself, had asked me to do this presentation at her friend's home in Pacific Heights. There would be about ten women, all parents of teens and young adults, grappling with modeling and management around money. Though I am not a proponent of working for free or bartering, I did donate my time, and you won't believe what happened. It was going to be a low-tech evening, so I handwrote my talking points and drove up to San Francisco.

We all sat together in a circle in the living room. I was really on fire that night and explained the prescription, the bottom-line behaviors, unapologetically. Everyone was startled by the content and one of them said, "What twenty-something at college doesn't have their parent's credit card?" They were all guilty, but I lovingly shared stories of hope, change, and powerful game-changing boundaries. Most importantly, they understood it was not too late and that with financial wellness, you can start fresh on any new day. We meandered over to the dining room table to share a meal. We discussed the nuances of what to say, when to deliver the messaging, and one parent confessed,

"My son is graduating in a few months and wants to move to New York City after college. He's fully expecting us to pay his rent and bills while he looks for a job. I can't afford that and we haven't talked about how much or for how long!" Longtime friends, the other moms laughed nervously and with recognition. I responded soberly, saying she needed to get straight with her money first. *Gasp!* So she could figure out what worked for her and communicate from that honest, grounded place. The woman sitting on my left said, "You should write a book! I want your book!" It turns out that lovely Hannah had a long career in publishing. The rest was history, God's handiwork indeed. My follow-up email was buried in her inbox for six months, but she responded. Hannah generously offered to coach me through the book proposal process and educated me on the publishing industry along the way. I was floored and emotional and so utterly grateful for the series of events and people that ushered me to this moment. At the end of our work together, Hannah also introduced me to my now agent Jen Newens.Jen and I quickly discovered our connection to at the intersection of Bay Area tennis and education. I taught her niece first grade at The Berkeley School and had long known her sister, Signy, from tennis. Signy and I first met at John Gardiner's Tennis Ranch in Carmel Valley back in the '90s when she was my counselor and coach. I mean, you can't make this up! It really proves that the Law of Attraction is a gray, circular, multidirectional, ebbing-and-flowing kind of deal. Miracle!

Now that I have a thorough understanding of child development from earning a kindergarten-through-eighth-grade teaching credential, a master's degree in educational technology, ten years of classroom teaching experience including some time at Bing Nursery School—Stanford's world-renowned preschool—ten years of parenting my own children, counseling with parenting experts, and reading innumerable books on parenting and positive discipline, I feel very confident in the following assertions. Here are the five best personal finance tips for sturdy parenting and preventing your loved ones from becoming my clients. The prescription for raising financially healthy teens and young adults is:

No Credit Cards
Understand the Emotions and Dynamics at Play
Pay Bills with Transparency
Limit Spending Money
Support Simple Budgets

1. No Credit Cards. Yes, you read that correctly. I am recommending you take back the credit card(s), immediately. Spending on credit is inappropriate for someone with a developing brain. The prefrontal cortex, the area responsible for executive functioning and decision-making, is not fully developed until the age of twenty-five. Alcohol and cannabis (pot) use can damage the maturing prefrontal cortex and make your young adult children even more susceptible and impulsive than they already are. One client shared with me, "My dad paid off my credit cards multiple times throughout my twenties and it was *not* helpful!"

Another client in her fifties was in a thick money fog. Her husband was unemployed, and she worked as many hours as she could including overtime, but they were running out of money between paychecks and draining savings at a startling pace. At my suggestion, she hired a bookkeeper to help her categorize her family's credit card spending that year to date. Up until that point, her two children, nineteen and twenty-one, had unlimited, unchecked use of the family credit card. My client was floored, *absolutely shocked,* at the volume of transactions for food delivery to their dorm rooms when both kids were on meal plans at college, not to mention their bar charges, weekend travel spending, and extraneous shopping. It was a colossal but necessary wake-up call for the whole family.

Young adults—those under the age of twenty-five—need to learn how to discern between needs and wants. Picture your kids walking through a maze blindfolded. They have to figure out how to navigate through, right? Realistic financial decision-making is possible only when coupled with firm boundaries, like limited funds in a checking account. Spending money provides a powerful dopamine hit for the brain and can become its own addiction too. Please don't allow your teens and young-adult children to start a habit of overspending at this vulnerable age. Managing a checking account, which contains actual money, gives your kids skin in the game. Within the safety and confines of a straightforward checking account, they have the opportunity to practice managing the ins and outs, an essential life skill. Handing them a credit card is like giving them a car that never runs out of gas or power.

I know what you're thinking: *What about emergencies*? Long gone are the days when we supposedly had to have a credit card to pay for the tow truck on the side of the road when the car broke down. As a parent today, you are virtually always reachable if something comes up. And if you're concerned that your child needs to start building credit, simply add them as an authorized user on your credit card account. And don't give them a card or the number. This is assuming, of course, that you're a healthy credit card user who never carries a balance for long or incurs interest charges. Take your child's hand and walk them back over the bridge from the land of magical thinking and credit cards to reality, the land of honesty, presence, and debit cards. Just say no!

Financial Psychology Research

College students report they learned more about credit cards from their parents than from any other source, and the more a parent was involved with their child, the lower that child's credit card balance.

2. Understand the Emotions at Play. You must do your own research and inner work about the emotions that are coming up and the dynamics at play during this transition. It's an emotional time. I see you and acknowledge that your baby is growing up. For eighteen years (or longer), you have been their nurse, cook, driver, cleaner, teacher, personal assistant, organizer, life coach, travel agent, researcher, and laundress, all while volunteering and working! They may be moving out of your home. It's a big deal and a rite of passage for you both, but watch your *need to be needed.* Most parents are enablers by definition. We make systems work, manage and protect. We're competent and often make ourselves indispensable. All humans are interdependent by nature; just make sure the scales don't tip into disordered behavior like financial enabling and dependency. There are physical, emotional, and mental risks for enablers, including stress-related illnesses,

resentment, martyrdom, delusion, and even low self-worth. Perhaps even more dangerous, the risks for your teen or adult children include little experience actually living, loneliness, unhappiness, stunted development, dampened passion and creativity, reliance on others for nonwork income, difficulty with intimacy, poor coping, overconfidence, and limited future choices. Accept that you won't be there forever, and it's time for your young-adult children to learn practical life skills, develop independence, and experience the wholeness of the human experience.

What you can do is punctuate and celebrate this time with professional pictures, visits, frequent check-ins, FaceTime, and sharing about new experiences—yours and theirs. Differentiation is a normal, natural part of family life that may not always feel comfortable, but your resistance to letting go could handicap your child. Remember, our number one job as parents is to raise functional adults. Check out the groundbreaking parenting books *How to Raise an Adult* by Julie Lythcott-Haims and *The Blessing of a Skinned Knee* by Wendy Mogel, among others, at sfmoney-coach.com/resources if you want a deeper dive on this topic.

3. <u>Pay Bills with Transparency.</u> All of the parents of young adults I have worked with ask, "What about paying their bills?" I understand that most parents strive to provide shelter, safety, and even some comforts. And many families continue offering financial support to their young-adult children throughout their twenties and sometimes beyond. Make a plan with clear agreements about the family dole. Start with an inventory and make a complete list of the current support: cell phone, Amazon

purchases, clothes, food, car/gas/insurance, Uber/Lyft/taxis, health insurance/health-care expenses (including therapy), family streaming and tech services, and the most expensive ones, which are often travel, tuition, and rent. Once you've done some of your own financial organization, you need to do some soul-searching on that monthly and annual number per child. Ask yourself honestly, can you continue to give that level of support? Will you feel happy and peaceful about providing that dollar amount for the next year? Five years? Longer? How does your spouse or partner feel about it? What does your financial advisor say? Once you get oriented, it's your prerogative to decide what, when, and how to wean your young-adult child over time, if necessary. I am not suggesting that you spontaneously cut the cord, but you have arrived at a teachable moment.

Here is a potential script for disentangling financially:

> "Let's have a family meeting. I've been looking at my money, and I want to share what I've discovered with you. Right now, you're receiving $5,000 of family support each month. These are posttax dollars, which means I need to earn about $7,800 per month to give that to you. Nothing is changing today, but in three months, I'd like to reduce the monthly support number to $4,000 (and so forth). Let's talk about what questions you have and what this will mean for you."

The details will vary with every situation, but make an explicit plan including allotted money, spending limits, and a time frame (usually thirty to sixty days to start), then meet to reflect and review. Is this working for me? Is this working for you? Is this working for our relationship? If anyone answers "no," you may need help from a neutral third party to renegotiate the plan to terms everyone can live with.

4. Limit Spending Money. In addition to the monthly support for bills and the fixed and discretionary expenses listed above, what's honest and realistic for giving additional spending money? Young adults are inundated, 24/7, with images of great-looking, well-dressed people with all the things that teens and young adults covet. Whether it's their actual friends posting edited pictures of their best lives or models and celebrities they follow on social media, there is tremendous focus on outward appearance and pressure to *keep up with the Joneses*. But let's get real. Do they really need to color their hair at this age or get high-end skin care or have new outfits for every special event? Are you funding a lifestyle that's practical for a young adult? Is it aligned with your values or their demands? Of course, like you, I want them to have fun and enjoy life and be young and feel happy. And your financial life, as the one providing support or gifts, needs to have integrity. Does your child work? Can they earn more or supplement their own spending money? I know it can feel difficult and humbling to pull back what has been readily available, but what good comes from your child spending double their take-home pay with your help? Of course, you can still give gifts for birthdays, holidays, and other special occasions within reason, but in terms of monthly "foolish money," less is more. For example, your child will

have more awareness and consciousness if given $200 per month for spending money rather than $2,000 at the beginning of a semester.

5. Support Simple Budgets. For starters, if you're providing the funds, you must have access to their bank account. Help them create a spending plan (budget) on a shared Google spreadsheet, or—I know it sounds crazy—you could set one up by hand on paper together. Start with a list of how much money they have (bank account balances and cash), their bills, their wish list items/fun ideas, and possible miscellaneous spending in detail. If they can't manage $200 or $2,000 of spending money, imagine what would happen with more. If they run out of money, make them wait. Trust me, they will beg, whine, complain, get under your skin, trigger you, and try to wear you down just like they did when they were toddlers. Don't give in. Communicate that there are no loans, no extra money to cover X, Y, or Z that came up, and most of all, don't give in behind your spouse's back. Even as young adults, they're still sponges and watching the way you parent and handle not only consumption, but stress, as well. Your ability (or lack thereof) to cope with debt, and your money habits and skills, will be passed down, so make sure you're in good shape! The stakes are high and you need to be aware of the messages you're communicating. To strengthen the cycle of accountability, at the end of every month, help them review what happened to their money in detail. This is the perfect time for them to learn how to track the difference between the budget and actuals—in other words, reality.

Here's a scary story in this realm. Not one, but two of my clients reached out with eerily similar situations. Both women were in their sixties and divorced, lived on opposite coasts, and did not know each other. They were both 100 percent dependent on their fathers who, by this point, were in their nineties. These women lived with and took care of their fathers 24/7 and should certainly have been compensated for that job. However, both of them had dipped into the gray area, and each presented a neat calculus of their fathers' social security deposits, pensions, tax refunds, and any other assets their fathers had. It was difficult to discern the right allocation of funds and what appropriate pay would look like, since both fathers were also providing housing and paying for their utilities, cell phones, and car expenses, and the lines were very blurred. The real problem was that neither woman had a plan for income after her father passed away. While there might be some cash on hand and other limited funds leftover at the time of death, there was a zero percent chance either woman's inheritance would last them another thirty years of life. Both women had given up their careers for the caretaking role and maintained somewhat extravagant lifestyles, with expenses like renovations and pricey self-care retreats when they did take a break. They were both somewhat circling the drain, trying to manipulate the math such that they would *be okay*.

In my coaching, I started at square one with suggestions and gave them the same exact advice as I've outlined above in the prescription for teens and young adults, plus one glaringly obvious extra part: "You need a job. It's time for you to earn your own money again." They were stuck, though, in the around-the-clock job and anticipatory grief was setting in. I provided coaching and said things with kindness that I knew were difficult to hear. Coincidentally, my work with both of them started and concluded around the same time. I wonder how their stories would have ended if they had better access to financial education at a younger age. I wondered what lesson the Universe was teaching me. I think it was for me to pass on this message to *you*. Raising financially healthy kids needs to be a top priority for their mid-twenties launch plan.

If these suggestions prove difficult or even impossible for you to initiate, then I invite you to explore your own relationship with money and what's coming up around this. And if you, as their parent, can't be their guide and teacher in this area, then outsource the job to a professional. Someone's got to help your young adult lay the foundation for developing and mastering basic personal finance skills so they don't end up in my office later in life, facing serious consequences. Remember, the very best thing you can do for yourself and your young-adult children is learn how to have good conversations about money.

Advanced Life + Money

"We're all just walking each other home."
—Ram Dass, Psychologist
and spiritual leader

An elder close to me missed an opportunity to visit with her own sister, likely for the last time in her life, because neither of them was willing to talk about money. More than eighty years of unspoken family expectations around money were convoluted by past regrets, assumptions, mistaken agreements, and financial dependence. If only one or both of them had been brave and vulnerable and brought up the fraught topic. A script like the one belowcould save relationships and give love and closure a chance. Sadly, these women never got a chance to say goodbye or apologize, as one of them passed away in her sleep a couple of weeks later.

Enough of my clients were clueless about their aging parents' financial situations that I contacted my chaplain friend, Amanda. We dug into what's most important as you approach the end, and she created the following script. If the answers to these questions have not been freely given by aging family members, it's your responsibility to initiate a conversation. Someone has got to bring it up! Here are some questions to consider.

Advanced Life + Money Questions

Thank you for taking the time to talk with me about your finances! Let's get started.

1. Do you have:
    - A will or living will?
    - A power of attorney?
    - An advanced health-care directive?
    - A physician's order for life-sustaining treatment (POLST)?
    - A living trust?
    - Long-term care insurance?
    - A list of all cash, checking, savings, credit card, and investment accounts?
    - Annuities or other liquid assets for care support?
    - A financial advisor?
    - An estate attorney or elder-law attorney?
2. May I have copies? Where are these documents and the related contact information located? Can we have a meeting to go over them?

If the elder is at least eighty years old (or younger, if needed), request that you, the trustee, or the guardian of the estate be added to their bank accounts.

3. What is your vision for housing and medical care in your older years? What are your plans when you can no longer take care of yourself? How will you pay for it? What kind of care will you want as your capacities diminish? Who will oversee helping you access more care as you need it?
4. What do you envision for your funeral/celebration of life?
5. What is on your "bucket list"?
6. Do you want or need help managing your finances now (bill paying, mail, paperwork, and online systems)? How will we know when it's time to step in and help you manage your finances in the future?
7. How are you planning for your own death spiritually and mentally? Have you read any books? Talked to a spiritual leader, friends who are dying, or a therapist?
8. Is there anything you hoped we would talk about today, but didn't?

You can download the Advanced Life + Money Questions at sfmoneycoach.com/downloads.

Personal finance sometimes feels as intense as confronting our own mortality, but in the vein of being of service, having good intentions, and trying to help, why not try? When you approach a loved one to talk about their advancing life and related money questions, they will say one of three things: "Yes," "No," or "Not now."

Chapter Five

Long-Term Financial Wellness

I want to reiterate my belief that how you do money is how you do life. Long-term financial wellness requires continuous self-awareness and a commitment to rigorous honesty. *At Peace with Money* is a guidebook for having a dynamic relationship with money. The invitation is to consistently examine your cash flow, reevaluate your core values and goals periodically, create a retirement plan, explore right-brain financial tools and exercises, be open to financial wellness as a spiritual practice, get help as needed, and continue studying and learning more about money for the rest of your life. Will you join me?

Remember, the steps for maintaining a healthy relationship with money are relatively simple, but they do require consistency. That is the hardest part! If you can set up a system and build the personal finance routines into your life, just once a week, that's a huge win. You've got this. From there, you can engage in big-picture lifestyle planning and analyzing; however, you can't skip the foundation. There are no shortcuts on the financial wellness journey. Slow and steady is best. With accurate tracking and conscious cash-flow management in place, you might even find yourself with *more* time to read, listen to personal finance podcasts, take a course, have necessary conversations, work with a professional, and find other ways to expand your financial literacy.

My personal definition of financial literacy includes an understanding of:

- Spending plans (a.k.a., budgets)
- The basics of debt management, taxes, and savings
- Investing for long-term security
- The emotional, spiritual, and psychological sides of money
- A professional financial support team
- Tools and resources to continue learning

Three Stages of Wealth

Author and wealth coach Barbara Huson describes the three stages of wealth as Survival, Stability, and Wealth/Affluence. Based on two decades of personal and professional research, here is my understanding of each stage and how people at all stages navigate this limited resource.

Survival

You know you're in survival mode when you stash unopened mail, count the days and hours until the next deposit, and run out of money faster than expected. You're riddled with fear, negative thinking, and have crippling financial insecurity. You're truly living paycheck to paycheck, and the cycle of concern about money seems never ending.

People in Survival Mode:

- Carry balances on their credit cards.
- Spend inordinate amounts of time and energy moving money around.
- Feel regret and remorse about past financial decisions.
- Feel powerless and resigned about catching up.
- Owe back taxes or have overdue bills.
- Obsess yet avoid their money.
- Face the threat of collections and services being shut down.

Stability

You know you're financially stable when you are current with your taxes, have steady income, and pay your bills in full and on time every month. You live in housing that works. You're able to sustain savings and cover periodic expenses without using a credit card or freaking out.

Basic Milestones of Financial Stability:

- Thorough understanding of monthly and annual spending and earning
- Six months of living expenses set aside in a safety net savings account
- Regular contributions to retirement
- Appropriate insurance: health, home, car, life, and long-term care

Wealth/Affluence

The Merriam-Webster dictionary defines wealth as an abundance of valuable material possessions or resources. The archaic definition is well-being or prosperity. Wealthy people embody a sense of security and have the luxury of choice. These men and women have transcended daily and monthly concerns over bank account balances and are now giving back to themselves, their families, and society. There is an abundance of time, money, energy, and resources to make the world a better place. All basic financial needs are met, and there is more pleasure, self-care, and adventure on the calendar.

Act Like a Wealthy Person:

- Hire a certified financial planner or investment advisor.
- Strategize for periodic income.
- Have a will, trust, advanced health directive, and a durable power of attorney.
- Work with a CPA to optimize tax savings.
- Understand your parents' wills.
- Be educated on the details of your entire estate.
- Ensure that everyone in your family, across generations, is empowered with personal finance life skills and clear about the elders' end-of-life wishes.

There *is* a potential dark side to wealth. The danger zone for affluent people is excess. One of my high-net-worth clients, a single man, had twenty-six monthly magazine subscriptions but never made time to read even one. Affluent people usually have access to services, savings, investments, tax and business loopholes, and outright wealth accumulation that other people don't. They have an extraordinary opportunity and responsibility to channel this flow of energy for good.

Common Pitfalls of Affluent People:

- An unhealthy or unconscious relationship with money due to outsourcing, overdoing, and overwhelm
- Too much stuff, too many houses, and a loss of contact with simple, natural, connected, and meaningful experiences
- Entitlement that encroaches on their personal and professional relationships
- Severe loneliness

On my own adventure of financial wellness, I have experienced all of these stages of wealth at different times. After the pandemic, when my husband lost his job and along with it our family health insurance and LTIs (long-term incentives), we burned through our safety net and quickly slid back into survival mode. Of course, it is possible to resonate with the behaviors, experiences, and feelings from more than one stage of wealth at a time. Conflict and stress over money arises when the outside doesn't match the inside. Sometimes, people have all "the stuff" but are emotionally exasperated over their imbalanced life and simply can't enjoy it. Others have little to nothing and have joy, gratitude, and faith enough to add years to their life. The long-term financial wellness journey is about aligning your vision of financial and emotional security with your actions—*karma*. At last, peace of mind about money is possible.

Financial Support Team

If there's a single takeaway for you in this book, let it be this. The most powerful thing I've done in my journey with money is tell the truth to another person. My very first financial confidante was my dear friend, Ali. She happened to be a relationship counselor, so I knew she could *handle it* and keep my secrets. I told her facts about my financial life. How much I was making, how much I wanted to earn, what my upbringing was really like, the size of my debt, my creative strategies and elaborate plans for making ends meet, and the long list of things I didn't understand. Over time, I shared my breakthroughs and accomplishments too. She listened with love and reverence and patience and held a safe space for me to share in a vault of confidentiality, and my life was forever changed. It was this experience that set my entire financial wellness journey into motion. Opening up to a financial confidante (best financial friend) led me to hire a financial therapist, which inspired me to engage with a financial coach.

Ten years after graduating from college, twenty years after getting my first job, a friend suggested I contact the Financial Recovery Institute. There, I finally found the solution. From the first phone call with the founder, Karen McCall, to my first coaching appointment, I felt cared for, seen, heard, and understood. Immediately upon starting the financial recovery process while attending weekly appointments with my counselor and taking her suggestions, things started to shift, improve, and expand in every area of my life.

The depth of my fear and dysfunctional patterns had not been created overnight, nor was there a quick fix. However, I had my first financial accountability partner, someone to talk to about everything that came with the emotions and practicalities around money. In my coaching practice, I've seen other people's transformation with money begin in that initial consultation. People sometimes cry and sigh audible sounds of relief. It is very powerful to come out of isolation around money.

As the years passed, I have also received support from these various financial support team members. We truly cannot do this alone!

- Financial confidante/best financial friend (BFF)
- Financial therapist
- Money coach
- Bookkeeper
- Accountant (CPA)
- Business coach/mentor
- Fee-only certified financial planner (CFP)
- Family lawyer/estate attorney
- Life coach

How to Choose a Financial Advisor

There are countless financial advisors in the United States and around the world. Considering each person's personality, fee structure, communication style, brand, and small print is enough to make your head spin. To make things easier for you, here are my top five tips for choosing a financial advisor:

Trust
Referrals
Know What You Want

Research
Preparation

1. It's all about trust. You need to feel comfortable with your advisor, because 50 percent of a working relationship is about the services he or she can provide for you, and 50 percent of it is based on how you connect with the person. Are you inspired to meet with your advisor on a regular basis? Are you motivated to do the footwork necessary between appointments? Do you like and trust your advisor? The answer to all of these questions should be *yes*; otherwise, keep looking.
2. Get a personal referral. Find people in your immediate community whose relationship to money you respect. Ask them who they use for financial planning, taxes, investment advice, and estate planning. Ask them for details about what they like about the individual, the firm, and the service?
3. Know what you want. It is worthwhile to write down the qualities you are looking for in an advisor. Here are some to consider: warm, friendly, smart, licensed, convenient office hours and location, expertise in your areas of need, specific gender, and if they're easy to communicate with. It is equally important to know what your immediate goals are: to create a monthly budget, build sustainable periodic and safety net savings, design an annual plan, project your finances five to ten or more years out, receive investment advice, reallocate assets, plan for retirement, save for college, refinance your home, and so forth.
4. Do your research. Check out at least three different advisors whose services meet your needs. Read their

websites, read the paperwork they give you, look them up on Google, Yelp, LinkedIn, and seek out other reviews. Meet in person more than once, if possible, before you hire them.

5. Be Prepared. Here are some questions to consider, add your own, and make sure you ask all of them.

Do you offer a free consultation? How much time should I expect to commit to get the most benefit? What is your approach to [insert your current needs]? Who is your target audience? What is your fee structure, and how will this change over time? Are you a fiduciary (fee-only advisor)?

Your finances are deeply personal and should be treated with the utmost care and respect. You deserve to feel heard, empowered, and to receive customized services that meet your needs on your timeline. It is your responsibility to choose a financial advisor who you genuinely trust at a price that fits into your short- and long-term financial picture.

Money Affirmations

As simple as a deep breath, affirmations are words you think or say and believe to be true. You can use affirmations for anything you want to change in your life. Think of a situation that's causing problems for you and the resulting emotion. For example, "I don't have enough money—anxiety, fear. Rewrite a healthier, more productive version, and use this positive statement to reprogram your subconscious. Here are some examples for you to play around with:

- I am confident in my ability to make money.

- I am willing to see this differently.
- I always spend less than I earn.
- I love money and appreciate what it does for me.
- I am very optimistic about my financial future.
- I am financially and emotionally secure.
- I am paid what I am worth.
- I am passionate about my work.
- I have supportive, nurturing relationships.
- I like wealthy people.
- I am debt-free.
- I am financially free.
- I am resilient and able to bounce back when I make mistakes.
- I am filled with gratitude for the success I've achieved.
- I am delighted to delegate and set limits.
- I am attracting the perfect people to help me reach my goals.
- I love money.

Write Your Own Money Affirmations

1. Close your eyes and visualize what you want. Then, draw a picture or sketch an image of what you see.

    ____

    ____

    ____

    ____

    ____

2. Reread your personal finance goals. What inspiration or encouraging words come to mind? Always start an

affirmation with positive, present-tense words such as I can, I am, I do, I have, I feel, I love, and so on.

____

____

____

____

____

3. Say your affirmation over and over to integrate a new, healthy money soundtrack.
4. Read an affirmation when your old money scripts pop up or you are having a lot of unhappy or negative thoughts.
5. Look in the mirror and say your positive affirmations out loud.
6. Write your affirmations down in a notebook or journal.
7. Make a sign with your positive affirmations and hang it where you can see it every day, like your dresser, mirror, desk, fridge, computer desktop, or bulletin board.

You can download the Money Affirmations exercise at sfmoneycoach.com/downloads.

Carrie's Affirmations in 2025

I am empowered and smart with money.
I am actively building and sustaining multiple levels of savings.
I experience prosperity and abundance.
I am strong.
I can handle this.
I feel happy and confident with money.
I am at peace with money.

And so it is.

My Affirmations

Slowing down, taking deep breaths, and doing whatever it takes to remain in the present moment has helped improve my life and financial health. I recommend that all my clients read or say their money affirmations aloud every day. I believe this practice allows you to tap into the unlimited power of mindfulness.

Reflections

SF Money Coach started with humble beginnings. When I officially became certified as a financial coach back in 2010, all of my appointments were house calls. I would meet with people in their living rooms and at their kitchen tables. I remember my very first client saying, "I just want to have enough money that I don't need to think about it." I understood what she was trying to say and responded, "I hear you, and that's just it. The more money you have, the larger the responsibility and the higher your money consciousness needs to be."

For those first couple of years, I continued driving around from apartment to apartment, house to house, and office to office, dealing with parking in San Francisco, then subway delays in New York City, and constant, normal workday and family-life disruptions. As I got busier, it all became too much, but still incredibly conflict averse to this day, I was afraid to rock the boat. I dreaded saying, "For our next appointment, I need you to come to me." I worried my clients would vanish and my brand-new coaching practice would deteriorate. I also needed to find an appropriate office space. Yet, there came a time when there was no other option but to put boundaries in place. I may have lost a client or two during the transition, but I gained a formidable amount of self-esteem from the simple act of sharing my needs. Enough of my clients, and my new clients, followed suit. The more I practiced self-care around work, the more my business expanded.

In fifteen years of private practice, I have learned to tolerate rejection. I've grown to accept that I am not for everyone, and everyone is not for me. Amazingly, year after year, more and more of my ideal clients keep showing up, from all over the world. I have met the most incredible people from all walks of life. I love every one of them and their families. I am honored that I've been involved in clinical research and invited to speak at universities. I've enjoyed many professional development courses, attending conferences, and communing with my professional network. All this time, I've been inviting clients to practice mindfulness and self-reflection in their relationship with money, mostly because that's what I value in my own life. I know on a deep and personal level how a few simple concepts can change *everything*. The predicament of self-employment and a long-term journey of financial wellness has not been easy, but I wouldn't change a thing.

And then life happened. Throughout the first ten years of marriage, my husband, our family's primary breadwinner, got promotion after promotion. The firm he worked for in New York City paid for our move back to California, and he received a cost-of-living salary *increase* upon arriving in the Bay Area. Since he worked at two different publicly traded companies, we enjoyed stock options, healthy bonuses, and full savings accounts. We usually had several trips booked at once (travel and adventures are shared core values for us), including skiing with our kids—the ultimate luxury sport. I never thought I would struggle financially again until my husband got laid off in the fallout of the pandemic. As I write this, he's been unemployed for over two years, and it took us about that long to stabilize our family cash flow. While continuing to interview for full-time jobs, Andrew is building a consulting business from scratch, which will take time. I know many people have lost jobs since 2020, and the effects have been devastating.

My husband did receive a generous severance package including short-term health insurance coverage. Andrew had many new job opportunities come his way. Each interview process lasted for two months or longer—to no avail. All near misses. Always hopeful the next opportunity would pan out, we started paying $3,918 per month for COBRA health insurance coverage. When this *finally* became prohibitive, coupled with Andrew's tenth finalist rejection, we dealt with switching health insurance companies and everything that entailed for our family of four. Here's a partial list of other actions we took to reduce our spending:

- Applied for financial aid at our son's preschool and daughter's choir program
- Asked for a sliding scale rate from my yoga instructor
- Spent several school breaks at home on "staycations"
- Let go of our beloved nanny
- Humbly asked our parents for help contributing to our kids' public school and 529 college savings accounts
- Made peace with our unique housing situation (renting the first floor of his mother's house)
- Consigned unused household items like exercise equipment
- Bought used furniture and went thrifting for clothes
- Weighed the pros and cons of moving
- Canceled several media subscriptions
- Joined and became active in a local Buy Nothing group
- Handwrote a letter to my dentist requesting they remove a ninety-dollar appointment cancelation fee from my account due to our current hardship
- Traded supervising puppy play dates rather than paying for a dog walker

- Traded in my car to reduce monthly payments
- Took out a personal loan with 0 percent interest for a much-needed therapeutic couples retreat during these dark times
- Created a payment plan with the IRS to tackle back taxes
- Gave up my sanctuary home office/guest house to a permanent renter

I realize that these kinds of challenges and changes are first-world problems, but honestly, it's been a rocky time. Most significantly for me, in the fall of 2024, I returned to full-time work in education with the main purpose of providing health insurance benefits for my family. I'm working at a wonderful elementary school in my neighborhood and love getting out of the house every day. It was a *long* fifteen years of self-employment and working from home for this extrovert. And my colleagues, all educators, are just the best. They're smart, warm, open, and all share my passion for child development. I am essentially starting over in the field as a full-time guest teacher, a substitute on staff. Having a boss again, not to mention the whims of my students, has its ups and downs, but I am beyond grateful for the opportunity to work at this small school with a big heart. And I will do whatever it takes to help my family strike balance again.

> "In the end, only three things matter: how much you loved, how gently you lived, and how gracefully you let go of things not meant for you." —Buddha

Appendix

At Peace with Money Downloads

All downloads can be found at sfmoneycoach.com/downloads.

Financial Partnership Questions
Money Affirmations
Personal Finance Routines
Sample Budget Categories
Age-Appropriate Chore Chart
Personal Capital Exercise
Values Clarification Exercise
Advanced Life + Money Questions
Business Deductions: Easy and Official
Underearning Assessment

At Peace with Money Resources

All resources, websites, and links mentioned in the book, plus bonus material, can be found at sfmoneycoach.com/resources, including:

MEDITATION

Vipassana
HolosyncMBSR—Mindfulness-Based Stress Reduction

EXERCISES FOR SELF-AWARENESS

Multiple Intelligences for Adults and Strengths Survey
Character and Strengths Survey
Klontz Money Script Inventory-R (KSMI-R)
Klontz Money Behavior Inventory (KMBI)
Financial Health Scale (FHS)
Personality Assessor
Love, Apology, Anger, and Appreciation Language Quizzes

PARENTING

Articles

"Best Age for Kids to Start Doing Chores," *Psychology Today*
"Sparing Chores Spoils Children and Their Future Selves," *Boston Globe*
"Why Kids Who Do Chores Become Successful Adults," *Motherly*
"Kids Who Do Chores Are More Successful Adults," *Inc.*
"The Single Best Things Parents Can Do to Make Sure Their Kids Are Successful," *Business Insider*

Books

How to Raise an Adult by Julie Lythcott-Haims
The Blessing of a Skinned Knee by Wendy Mogel
The Spiritual Child by Dr. Lisa Miller

Additional Parenting Resources

Save/Give/Invest/Spend Money Bank
Greenlight Debit Card for Kids and Teens
Dr. Becky Kennedy, Parenting Coach

Janet Lansbury, Parenting Coach

COMPULSIVE SPENDING

Life-Energy Calculator
A Guide to Causes and Treatment
Stopping Overshopping
Money-Related 12-Step Programs: Codependents, Overspending, Gambling, Debtors, Business Debtors, or Bettors Anonymous

COUPLES

Gottman Institute
Love Languages Institute

ADVANCED LIFE

Five Wishes
The Conversation Project

DEBT MANAGEMENT

Debt Calculators: CNN and Undebt It
Snowball Method (useful for momentum)
Avalanche Method (saves on interest)
Take Charge America

INHERITANCE

Sudden Money Institute

Personal Finance 101 Master Class

https://www.sfmoneycoach.com/master-class

A comprehensive, self-paced, online course with twenty-five interactive mini lessons on the practical and emotional aspects of personal finance steeped in clinical research, cognitive and solution-focused therapy, and behavioral finance. Get up close and personal with Carrie Friedberg, the SF Money Coach and author of *At Peace with Money*, as she narrates the whole course by recorded video. The course includes a do-it-yourself (DIY) twenty-five-page editable PDF workbook with tools, exercises, and bonus material. Love pen to paper? You can order a beautifully bound workbook to be shipped directly to you.

Financial Wellness with Carrie Podcast

Psychology-informed financial coach and Financial Behavior Specialist®, Carrie Friedberg interviews experts on topics ranging from wealth building, earning, aging, happiness, conscious spending, the art of accountability, and much more. Carrie teaches individuals, couples, and small-business owners all over the world how to feel confident and intentional with their money.

Apple Podcasts - https://podcasts.apple.com/us/podcast/financial-wellness-with-carrie/id1618602007

Spotify - https://open.spotify.com/show/1UnRRBrkuO3GCiBpVANeaO

SOCIAL MEDIA

LinkedIn - https://www.linkedin.com/in/carriebirgbauer/

Instagram - https://www.instagram.com/sfmoneycoach/

Facebook - https://www.facebook.com/SFMoneyCoach

YouTube - https://www.youtube.com/channel/UC17bjhag8tSvy2_Celu1Uww

Pinterest - https://www.pinterest.com/sfmoneycoach/

Acknowledgments

Lucy (Bear Bear) and Max (Maxibu)—You two are the best gifts I have ever received. I waited a long time to meet you, but I *always* knew I would. I love you both with all my heart and soul. Good luck with this money stuff—I'm rooting for you!

Andrew (Ansie)—You are the most competent, loving, generous, patient, and accepting person I have ever met. I clearly won the husband lottery. Thank you for suggesting the title, visualizing the cover, helping me to make cuts and move around large sections, your astute line edits, and for your unwavering support of this dream along with my thousands of other "great ideas." Even if we're incompatible as doubles partners, I still choose you and will love you forever.

My Tribe of Women—My sister Beth and closest friends: Ali, Kristin, Hillary, Megan, Annie, Suzanne, Amanda (godmother to Max), Jen (twin cousin), Morgan, Shannon, Kate, and Lauren. A special thank-you to Leslie for being an early reader and a beta-tester and editor of my online course. You all continuously offer pure love and support beyond measure. Thank you for loving me throughout the relationship journey, helping me raise my children, encouraging me through dark times, and being infinite wells of inspiration. We've got this, mamas!

Sandra—Thank you for caring for my children from infancy to walking home from the bus alone. You held me up, taught me perseverance, and raised me as a mother. I learned so much from you and your gorgeous, feminine ways of managing a household and navigating relationships, parenthood, grief, health challenges, and faith. You're a domestic goddess and my career and this book would not have been possible without you. Your love is a beautiful gift and I miss you.

Ellie V.—You're a phenomenal role model for me: an athlete, fitness guru, vegan activist, and canine aficionado—not to mention CEO of your own company! You're a modern-day hero, my friend. Thank you for your friendship, tennis partnership, mentorship, and unbelievable generosity, which has taken my doubles, career, life, and writing to deeper levels than I knew imaginable.

My tennis and pickleball teammates—I love and admire each and every one of you. Thank you for being patient with me and for accepting me and my, at times, intensely dissociative, moody, and overly competitive ways. I learn from you every time we play. You are beautiful examples of grace, dignity, and respect on and off the court. I hope we can grow old and keep playing together.

My brothers, John and Peter—Thanks for helping educate me in the department of finance, for answering my money questions (repeatedly), explaining investment and legalese in ways I can understand, and for the spacious listening, grounded advice, and unconditional love.

My parents, Anne (mem. 2018) and Bruce—Mom, you're the first woman I ever noticed was "right with money." You always appreciated money and enjoyed spending it to provide happiness, beauty, safety, love, dreams realized, and wonder in the world. I miss you every day. Dad, I am so grateful that you modeled an unwavering commitment to the spiritual path from a very young age: faith, forgiveness, prayer, service, and unconditional love. The lessons you taught me about money are priceless. Work hard, be smart (frugal), and save, save, save! Thank you for everything you sacrificed to give me an extraordinary education, a chance at my athletic aspirations, and for showing me the world. I love you, Dad.

My mother-in-love, Sylvia—Words can't express how much I appreciate your incredibly generous support over the last decade. And thank you for sharing your beautiful home with my young family. You have wholeheartedly offered your time and energy taking care of our children and puppy, Luna, so I could work, play tennis, and spend quality time out of the house with your son. I learned the art of letting go from you.

My mentors—Bob Wood, Elli Findly, Terri DeLangis, Aishlin O'Coyle, Karen McCall, Mikelann Valterra, Barbara Huson, Ted Klontz, and Brad Klontz. Thank you for demonstrating how to work in the *invisible world* and for providing me with world-class education, accountability, and empowerment. Karen, step by step, you guided me in launching a business from scratch that survived two cross-country moves and two maternity leaves. My business thrived from day one and opened doors for me I never knew possible. I'm grateful for you! Each of you helped me transform my ownrelationship with money, discover my superpowers, and grow a business/passion/lifestyle beyond my wildest dreams. *You changed my life.*

My magical book people—Patrick, Laura, Ashley, Lindsay, and Hannah. Without a shadow of a doubt, our meeting and work together was God's handiwork. Thank you for your trust, love, grace, and generosity. You're each in my heart forever.

My literary godmother—Jen Newens at Martin Literary Management. I met you inside our amazing Bay Area community at the intersection of work, tennis, and education. I'm certain our meeting was divinely orchestrated and I am forever grateful for your guidance and expertise along the way. Thank you!

The Post Hill Press team—Debby Englander, thank you for being a champion of women being empowered with money and for taking a chance on me as a first-time author. And Caitlin Burdette, thank you for midwifing this book into being. Kate Post, editor extraordinaire, you are truly gifted. Thank you all for your sharing your expertise, attention to detail, and thoughtful suggestions that shaped *At Peace with Money* into a beautiful book. I am incredibly grateful to the entire team!

Bibliography

Beattie, Melody. *Codependent No More: How to Stop Controlling Others and Start Caring for Yourself.* Center City, MN: Hazelden Publishing, 1992.

Chapman, Gary. *The Five Love Languages: How to Express Heartfelt Commitment to Your Mate.* Chicago, IL: Northfield Publishing, 1995.

Dass, Ram, and Mirabai Bush. *Walking Each Other Home: Conversations on Loving and Dying.* Louisville, CO: Sounds True, 2018.

Mueller, Gerrit, and Erik Plug. "Estimating the Effect of Personality on Male and Female Earnings." *ILR Review* 60, no. 1 (2006): 3–22. https://doi.org/10.1177/001979390606000101.

Flanders Family Home Life. "Age-Appropriate Children's Chore Chart." Last modified July 18, 2024. https://www.flandersfamily.info/web/organization/printable-charts/#h-chore-charts.

Ingerman, Sandra. *Soul Retrieval: Mending the Fragmented Self.* San Francisco, CA: HarperOne, 2006.

Investopedia Team. "What Is an Asset? Definition, Types, and Examples." *Investopedia.* Accessed 2024. https://www.investopedia.com/terms/a/asset.asp.

Kemnitz, Randy, Bradley Klontz, and Kristy L. Archuleta. "Financial Enmeshment: Untangling the Web." *Journal of Financial Therapy* 6, no. 2 (2016): 4. https://doi.org/10.4148/1944-9771.1085.

Klontz, Brad, Sonya L. Britt, and Kristy L. Archuleta. *Financial Therapy: Theory, Research, and Practice.* New York, NY: Springer Publishing, 2014.

Klontz, Brad, and Ted Klontz. *Mind over Money: Overcoming the Money Disorders That Threaten Our Financial Health.* New York, NY: Crown Business, 2009.

Klontz, B. T., P. Sullivan, M.C. Seay, and A. Canale. "The Wealthy: A Financial Psychological Profile." *Consulting Psychology Journal: Practice and Research 67, no.* 2 (2015): 127–143. https://doi.org/10.1037/cpb0000027.

Klontz, Bradley T., Michael C. Seay, Paul Sullivan, and A. Canale. "The Psychology of Wealth: Psychological Factors Associated with High Income." *Journal of Financial Planning* 27, no. 12 (2014): 46–53. https://www.financialplanningassociation.org/article/journal/DEC14-psychology-wealth-psychological-factors-associated-high-income.

Klontz, Bradley T., Paul Sullivan, Michael C. Seay, and A. Canale. "The Wealthy: A Financial Psychological Profile." *Consulting Psychology Journal: Practice and Research* 67, no. 2 (2015): 127–143. https://doi.org/10.1037/cpb0000027.

McCall, Karen. *Financial Recovery: Developing a Healthy Relationship with Money.* Novato, CA: New World Library, 2011.

MI Oasis. "MI Oasis." Accessed 2024. https://www.multipleintelligencesoasis.org/.

Miller, Dr. Lisa. *The Spiritual Child: The New Science on Parenting for Health and Lifelong Thriving.* New York, NY: Picador Books, 2016.

Northern, J. J., W. H. O'Brien, and P.W. Goetz. "The Development, Evaluation, and Validation of a Financial Stress Scale for Undergraduate Students." *Journal of College Student Development* 51, no. 1 (2010): 79–92. http://dx.doi.org/10.1353/csd.0.0108.

Perry, V. G. and M.D. Morris. "Who Is in Control? The Role of Self-Perception, Knowledge, and Income in Explaining Consumer Financial Behavior. *Journal of Consumer Affairs* 39, no. 2 (2005): 299–313. https://doi.org/10.1111/j.1745-6606.2005.00016.x.

Prelec, Drazen, and Duncan Simester. "Always Leave Home Without It: A Further Investigation of the Credit-Card Effect on Willingness to Pay." *Marketing Letters* 12, no. 1 (2001):5–12.https://doi.org/10.1023/a:1008196717017.

Robin, Vicki and Joe Dominguez. *Your Money or Your Life: 9 Steps to Transforming Your Relationship with Money and Achieving Financial Independence.* New York, NY: Penguin Books, 2008.

Shakespeare, William. *The Tragedy of Hamlet, Prince of Denmark.* London: The Folio Society, 1954.

Stanny, Barbara. *Overcoming Underearning™: Overcome Your Money Fears and Earn What You Deserve.* New York, NY: Harper Business, 2005.

Valterra, Mikelann. "How to Set Your Fees—The Many Hours Behind the Hour." SeattleMoneyCoach. Accessed 2024. https://www.seattlemoneycoach.com/how-to-set-fees-hour/.

West, Thomas G. *Plato's Apology of Socrates: An Interpretation, With a New Translation.* Ithaca, NY: Cornell University Press, 1979.

About the Author

Photo Credit: Laura Hamilton

Carrie Friedberg was raised in Grosse Pointe, Michigan. She studied Buddhism at Trinity College in Connecticut before moving to San Francisco to attend the graduate school of education at University of San Francisco. In addition to earning a multiple subject teaching credential and masters degree, Carrie became a certified yoga instructor and started practicing Vipassana meditation and Mindfulness Based Stress Reduction (MBSR).

Carrie has been featured by the US News, *Forbes*, *New York Post*, MarketWatch, and *Oprah Magazine*. Carrie has consulted as a money coach with Visa, Macy's, SAP, WeWork, Airbnb, and Google. She was involved in financial psychology research at Kansas State University and presented financial wellness workshops at University of San Francisco, Santa Clara University, and University of California, Berkeley. Carrie is a first-time author and lives in Portola Valley, California with her husband, two children, and their beloved Havanese, Luna.